BFI FILM CLASSICS

. . . .

Edward Buscombe
SERIES EDITOR

Colin MacCabe and David Meeker
SERIES CONSULTANTS

Cinema is a fragile medium. Many of the great classic films of the past now exist, if at all, in damaged or incomplete prints. Concerned about the deterioration in the physical state of our film heritage, the National Film and Television Archive, a Division of the British Film Institute, has compiled a list of 360 key films in the history of the cinema. The long-term goal of the Archive is to build a collection of perfect showprints of these films, which will then be screened regularly at the Museum of the Moving Image in London in a year-round repertory.

BFI Film Classics is a series of books commissioned to stand alongside these titles. Authors, including film critics and scholars, filmmakers, novelists, historians and those distinguished in the arts, have been invited to write on a film of their choice, drawn from the Archive's list. Each volume presents the author's own insights into the chosen film, together with a brief production history and a detailed filmography, notes and bibliography. The numerous illustrations have been specially made from the Archive's own prints.

With new titles published each year, the BFI Film Classics series will rapidly grow into an authoritative and highly readable guide to the great films of world cinema.

Could scarcely be improved upon ... informative, intelligent, jargon-free companions.
The Observer

Cannily but elegantly packaged BFI Classics will make for a neat addition to the most discerning shelves.
New Statesman & Society

BFI FILM

CLASSICS

ANNIE HALL

·····················

Peter Cowie

BRITISH FILM INSTITUTE

bfi

BFI PUBLISHING

First published in 1996 by the
BRITISH FILM INSTITUTE
21 Stephen Street, London W1P 2LN

The British Film Institute exists
to promote appreciation, enjoyment, protection and
development of moving image culture in and throughout the
whole of the United Kingdom.
Its activities include the National Film and
Television Archive; the National Film Theatre;
the Museum of the Moving Image;
the London Film Festival; the production and
distribution of film and video; funding and support for
regional activities; Library and Information Services;
Stills, Posters and Designs; Research;
Publishing and Education; and the monthly
Sight and Sound magazine.

British Library Cataloguing-in-Publication Data
A catalogue record for this book is available from the British Library

ISBN 0–85170–580–4

Designed by
Andrew Barron & Collis Clements Associates

Typesetting by
D R Bungay Associates, Burghfield, Berks.

Printed in Great Britain by
The Trinity Press, Worcester

CONTENTS

· ·

Acknowledgments   *7*

Introduction   *9*

The Personal Side   *11*

The Origins of *Annie Hall*   *14*

The Adoration of Manhattan   *19*

Inside *Annie Hall*   *22*

Visual Invention   *46*

Cultural Stereotypes   *48*

A Perennial Appeal   *50*

Glossary of Cultural References   *53*

Notes   *59*

Credits   *60*

Bibliography   *62*

ACKNOWLEDGMENTS

I would like to thank Allen Eyles, Diane Jacobs and Peter Meyer, for their encyclopedic knowledge of American comedy, Woody Allen, and New York City respectively. Praise, too, for my wife Françoise, who has suffered a stream of broken weekends to accommodate the completion of this little book. And a dedication to our son, Robin, who at the age of three already loves Westerns.

The publisher would like to thank David Peterson for his generous help.

Diane Keaton and Woody Allen

INTRODUCTION

. . . .

Some decades stare us in the face with defiance. The 20s, with their financial woes and artistic energy, or the 60s, rebelling against the status quo in everything from politics to pop music and couture. The 50s appeared austere and bland at the time, yet they produced Ingmar Bergman and Federico Fellini, two of Woody Allen's personal idols.

Perhaps the 70s have not yet assumed a shape and a flavour all their own. Lethargic in a Europe exhausted from the 'events' of '68 and their aftershock, the decade would prove more exciting in the United States. Feminism seized the high ground, everyone seemed to have a *shri* and a shrink, drugs brought a whiff of mischief to any social conclave, and the science of navel-gazing reached new heights.

Smack in the midst of the 70s, Woody Allen wrote and shot *Annie Hall*. With one bound he joined the pantheon of American directors, although his stature as a comedian was already assured thanks to hits like *Bananas*, *Sleeper*, *Play It Again*, *Sam*, and *Love and Death*.

Annie Hall (1977) happens to be one of the funniest pictures made in America since World War Two. Groucho Marx, who died on the first day of the year, and Charlie Chaplin, who passed away on one of the last, would both have been proud to sign such a film. Although it had opened in springtime, its reputation had not faded by the time Academy members came to vote the following February. *Annie Hall* won the Oscars for Best Picture, Best Director, Best Actress and Best Screenplay. Allen himself was nominated for Best Actor, but lost to Richard Dreyfuss for *The Goodbye Girl*. The film broke five Manhattan house records in its first weekend, earned $12 million in rentals at the US box-office (in a year when *Star Wars* and *Rocky* dominated the charts), and found appreciative audiences around the world. *Love and Death*, Allen's previous release, earned just $6,875,000 in rentals in the United States. In today's money, the international box-office gross for *Annie Hall* would exceed $100 million.

If the 70s can be assessed with increasing certainty as a decade of renaissance in American film, Woody Allen stands apart as having the finest talent to amuse (*pace* Mel Brooks). For Robert Benayoun, he is 'the only comic of international renown who can be described as an intellectual; and far from wearing out his welcome, he has never ceased to entertain his public with shrewd and playful observations.'[1]

Five Easy Pieces, with its poignant loss of hope and its grimace in the face of a crass society, had set the tone for the years ahead. Cassavetes, Coppola, Scorsese, Altman, Mazursky and de Palma each more or less presented a dark mirror to the 70s' soul. Films like *The Conversation*, *All the President's Men*, *Chinatown* and *Three Days of the Condor* reflected the political paranoia in the wake of Watergate.

By the time that *Annie Hall* appeared, on 20 April 1977, Hollywood was entering a period of change and self-scrutiny. The producer David Begelman had been found cashing cheques illegally at Columbia Pictures. Roman Polanski had been accused of having underage sex and had to flee the United States. Francis Ford Coppola was mortgaging the smoke from his house in order to save *Apocalypse Now* from oblivion. And one month later, on 25 May, the opening of George Lucas's *Star Wars* would herald an era of visceral action and adventure films built on old-fashioned values and exerting few demands on the minds of their audience.

Woody Allen's output during this period covers a remarkable range of form and content: *Bananas*, *Everything You Always Wanted to Know About Sex (But Were Afraid to Ask)*, *Sleeper*, *Love and Death*, *Annie Hall*, *Interiors* and *Manhattan*. Seven features in ten years, plus of course a scintillating appearance in Herbert Ross's *Play It Again, Sam* (written for the stage and screen by Allen himself), and a more sombre role in Martin Ritt's *The Front*. Diane Jacobs has commented that '*Annie Hall* is fundamentally neither timely nor realistic. In sharp contrast to such contemporary works as Michael Ritchie's 1977 *Semi-Tough*, Paul Mazursky's 1978 *An Unmarried Woman*, and Claudia Weill's 1978 *Girlfriends*, Allen observes but never stresses current social issues: never posits feminism (any more than as a narrative crisis), for instance, as "the reason why" something does or doesn't happen between a man and a woman.'[2]

Most filmgoers remember *Annie Hall* with a smile and a chuckle. For Allen himself, however, the film marked a career staging-post, even a departure from his previous work. It gave him the courage to pursue more serious, substantial themes while giving vent to the personal complexes that hitherto he'd aired only to live audiences as a stand-up comedian.

This was also the first time that he had paid homage to his home town, New York. The spirit of that city and, specifically among the five boroughs, of Manhattan and Brooklyn, has dominated a majority of his seventeen features since *Annie Hall*.

Every film in a 'contemporary' setting must lose some of its tang and relevance beyond its sell-by date. Some of the cultural references in *Annie Hall* no longer raise a laugh with anyone under forty; and some of its technical gimmicks look a trifle twee. But the verbal foreplay and the relaxed acting have endured, along with the seamless, swivelling drift of the narrative.

THE PERSONAL SIDE
. . . .

Most of the interesting ingredients of Woody Allen's life and personality can be gleaned from a study of his films, apart from his skill at playing the saxophone and the commitment he has given to jazz (note how the sea-deep melancholy of *September* is immeasurably enhanced by its jazz music on the soundtrack).

The paradox lies in his willingness to expose his innermost thoughts and complexes on screen, while leading an almost reclusive existence in New York. He may brush aside autograph hunters while dining at favourite restaurants like Elaine's or playing at Michael's Pub, but he does appear at the occasional party (for example, the one hosted by book publishers Harry N. Abrams in late 1995 for the launch of Brian Hamill's still photos of Allen's films). He may refuse to attend film festivals, even Cannes, to promote his work, and yet he has worked on location in Italy, France, Hungary aa well as California, his least favourite state of mind. He never shared a common apartment with Mia Farrow, but when she and he fought for custody of some of their children in 1992, Allen threw reticence to the winds and did not shirk the required court appearances. At the time he made *Stardust Memories*, at the end of the 70s, he resented the notion that his private relationships, by being shown on screen, could be applauded by audiences.

The clue to such contradictions can be found in the profession he has embraced from the earliest days: stand-up comedy. He likes making people laugh, and he even enjoys doing so in public, standing behind a mike, on a stage or, in the case of films like *Annie Hall*, addressing the audience in close-up. Eric Lax, in his excellent biography of Woody Allen,[3] has traced his career from sending in one-liners to comedian columnists in New York, to long and lucrative tours on the road, across the nation.

For a time, live sketches seemed to flow from his typewriter more easily than film concepts. The screenplay for *What's New Pussycat?* did not reach the screen as Allen had hoped. The unorthodox was rendered conventional, and the offbeat became cliché. Allen's reputation in cabaret brought him the offers, both as writer and actor. Not until *Take the Money and Run* in 1969, however, could he attach his name to a film with some reasonable measure of pride. Even that picture stuttered at the start of its run, and only picked up steam after being championed by *New York Times* critic Vincent Canby.

Just as a writer needs an understanding publisher and editor, so a film-maker depends on a good studio and an intelligent producer. Allen found both quite early in his career. United Artists, headed by Arthur Krim, gave him a three-picture contract after *Take the Money and Run*, and he remained under their aegis until he followed Krim and his associates to Orion Pictures in 1980. And his agents, Jack Rollins and Charles H. Joffe, became his producers, leaving him free to concentrate on the creative side of his work.

In the early 90s, *Variety* published an unflattering analysis of Woody Allen's box-office history, showing how much the studios had lost on his films over the years. Some of his chamber films, his serious dramas, have failed to attract even a modest public. Other films, like *Sleeper, Annie Hall, Manhattan, Hannah and Her Sisters*, and *Husbands and Wives*, have performed well. By the mid-90s, however, Allen was attracting a domestic gross of between $10 million and $15 million for a new film, whatever kind of release the distributors opted to give it. In an era when several films breach the $100 million barrier each year, that remains a modest figure. Yet Allen's work consistently out-performs even the best of the independent productions in the US.

His three most recently released works, *Manhattan Murder Mystery, Bullets over Broadway* and *Mighty Aphrodite*, have been pre-sold abroad for considerable sums. Since the late 70s, his films have found large audiences in Europe, which Allen himself accepts as a factor contributing to his survival as an auteur in the United States.

If any single work can be regarded as Allen's breakthrough into popular acceptance, then it must be *Play It Again, Sam*. Ironically, the film version of this stage play by Allen was directed by Herbert Ross, but so faithful was Ross to the spirit and letter of the play, and so forceful was Allen's performance as the would-be Bogart, that for most audiences it *was* a film by Woody Allen. Diane Keaton featured as his girlfriend, and Tony Roberts as his sidekick (revelling in a typical Allen running gag, that of leaving a phone number where he can be reached at all times). If the fantasy element of *Play It Again, Sam* prefigured such 'illusionist' films as *Zelig* and *The Purple Rose of Cairo*, then its New York wise-cracking dialogue seems in retrospect like a dry run for *Annie Hall* and *Manhattan*.

Bananas, released in 1971 and notorious for having introduced to the world the talents of Sylvester Stallone, runs at breakneck speed, rivalling the Marx Brothers with its profusion of visual gags, verbal asides and outrageous satire. The 'banana' republic would never be the same again. *Sleeper*, built on the Rip Van Winkle principle, raids the same slapstick tradition, and was the first film that Allen wrote with Marshall Brickman. When they approached United Artists for money to make *Annie Hall*, the success of *Sleeper* weighed decisively in their favour.

Even early in his career, Allen experimented with comic pace and idiom. *Everything You Always Wanted to Know About Sex...* derived from a straightforward manual by Dr David Reuben that swept the bestseller lists. By retaining the textbook's questions, and inventing the answers, Allen fashioned a film worth more than the sum of its episodes.

Love and Death, made the year before *Annie Hall*, emphasised the talents of Allen and Keaton as a comic duo. In this parody of Russian literature (*War and Peace* most notably, although *Crime and Punishment* is not far off), Allen's fondness for cultural references takes flight: Bergman, Mozart, Kafka, Eisenstein (Prokofiev's music embellishes the soundtrack), Sartre, and even one of Allen's favourite Bob Hope vehicles, *Monsieur Beaucaire*. With its fixation on themes like the quest for God, the fear of death, the fragile nature of love, and the significance of morality, *Love and Death* presents in absurdist form the dilemmas that haunt Allen's sombre films (*Interiors, September, Another Woman, Shadows and Fog*).

A film like *Interiors*, made immediately after *Annie Hall*, pries beneath the protective integument of laughter to reveal the melancholy that suffuses so many urban lives. The severity of its decor and the rigour of its technique evoke not just Ingmar Bergman and Carl Dreyer but also painters like Edvard Munch and Edward Hopper. Allen's satiric nature cannot remain bound for long, however, and colours the splendid scene in *Interiors* when Maureen Stapleton arrives like a gust of vulgar wind in the sterile world of E. G. Marshall's Arthur and his family.

Throughout the intervening two decades, Woody Allen has refused to rest on his laurels. Some films, like *A Midsummer Night's Sex Comedy*, *Manhattan Murder Mystery*, *Bullets over Broadway* and *Mighty Aphrodite*, do not tax the intelligence of the faithful, while others are so distilled and intense that they release their riches only after repeated viewings: *September*, *Crimes and Misdemeanours*, *Alice*... Then there are the films in which Allen experiments with his medium, creating witty and unfamiliar conjunctions with the aid of special effects: *Zelig*, *The Purple Rose of Cairo*, *Oedipus Wrecks* – or *Shadows and Fog*, with its conscious pastiche of German expressionist cinema.

The common theme concerns what the Swedish writer Hjalmar Söderberg called 'the desires of the flesh and the incurable loneliness of the soul'. Allen's characters (and especially those played by himself) strive for companionship; they may be surrounded by other human beings, but their attempts at communication lead to misunderstanding and failure. Fantasy serves as a refuge from the drudge of daily existence. This can take the form of a flight into history, into personal memories, or into the lore of cinema itself (*The Purple Rose of Cairo*).

Like many of the great European directors, Woody Allen abandons his films to the stream the moment they are completed. He often rejects them in disgust; he begged United Artists not to release *Manhattan*, even offering to make a film for free if they would comply with his request. Disappointed with the final result, Allen says, 'I think that one year ago, I was sitting in my bedroom and I had this great idea for a film that was beautiful and everything was so great. And then, little by little, I wounded it, in writing, in casting, in shooting, in editing, in mixing it, I want to get rid of it.'[4].

THE ORIGINS OF 'ANNIE HALL'

In 1974, Allen completed shooting *Love and Death* on locations in Europe and began discussing a new screenplay with Marshall Brickman, who had written *Sleeper* with him three years earlier. In fact the new film, provisionally entitled *Anhedonia*, would be an expanded version of the murder mystery he and Brickman had been discussing when *Love and*

Death came along to displace it. Now it would contain 'glimpses of problem childhood, career, and love experiences to the ends of portraying a successful middle-aged man incapable of experiencing pleasure'.[5] In psychiatry the term 'anhedonia' means precisely that: an inability to enjoy.

Marshall Brickman evokes the collaboration in his own droll way:

> I recall countless conversations on divers subjects: dialogs pirouetting and leaping from the Holocaust to Bertolt Brecht to Henry Youngman to the Essential Nature of the Novelistic Form, specifically the Novel of Memory, and is there a Cinematic Equivalent; to why girls with very large breasts are always sexy no matter what. ...
>
> The notion of taking the script of *Annie Hall* – or, more frighteningly, just the idea for the movie – to a rational studio head [...] and requesting millions of dollars to realize it on the screen is sufficient to induce a kind of nightmarish panic, even years after the movie was made and released.[6]

Brickman had met Woody Allen in the mid-60s in Greenwich Village. He had played banjo in a folk group managed by Jack Rollins and Charlie Joffe, Allen's agents and managers. Brickman chattered away while the rest of the group were tuning up 'because, he says, he could talk and tune up a little faster than the others'.[7] Writing about *Annie Hall* for the release of a laser disc version in 1990, Brickman recalls that he tended at the time 'to be more deliberate, concerned with structure, symmetry, construction: *form* – the refuge of the novitiate. Woody would graciously endure my endless exhortations to logic and plausibility and then casually suggest that perhaps the way to get the character out of the room would be, say, to have him flap his arms and fly out the window.'[8]

It was a genuine collaboration, similar to that of Mario Puzo and Francis Ford Coppola on *The Godfather*. 'Marshall and I spoke and spoke and worked out the plot and worked out the details. Then he went away and I wrote the draft. Then he would see it and make comments on it, tell me what he liked and what he disliked. We went over the draft together.'[9]

Quite how the crime story element vanished from *Annie Hall*, only to reappear to a lesser degree in *Stardust Memories* and to a greater degree in *Manhattan Murder Mystery*, is difficult to establish. Various factors came into play. The character of Annie Hall herself grew like Topsy, spun from Allen's memories of his affair with Diane Keaton between 1969 and 1972. The actress was born Diane Hall, but adopted her mother's maiden name, Keaton, because there was already another performer registered as Diane Hall in Actors' Equity.

Then Woody Allen himself would turn forty in December 1975, and felt the change of life upon him. 'I reached some kind of a personal plateau where I felt I could put the films that I had done in the past behind me,' he recalls.[10] He had some new colleagues in his crew, notably Gordon Willis, whose work on *The Godfather* films had brought him to the front rank of Hollywood cinematographers. Willis assured him, among other things, that he could have his actors speaking lines out of shot, that every line of dialogue did not have to be spoken into camera. He accompanied Allen on the time-consuming hunt for locations, along with art director Mel Bourne. One day in Brooklyn, they suddenly saw the roller-coaster, with Alvy's childhood house nestling beneath its curves, and realised that Alvy's memories had to start there rather than in Allen's own Flatbush birthplace.

Diane Keaton knew Willis from the long shooting schedules on *The Godfather* and its sequel. Allen she had met at the age of 23, when he cast her in the stage version of *Play It Again, Sam*. Apart from appearing in *Hair* on Broadway, Keaton had then done nothing of note, and her first screen role would be in *Lovers and Other Strangers* (1970). Although her special beauty and downtrodden wife would become familiar to *Godfather* audiences, it was Woody Allen who shaped forever her eccentric comedienne image for the 70s. By the time of *Annie Hall* she had already acted opposite him in three films: *Play It Again, Sam*, *Sleeper* and *Love and Death*. Less than six months after *Annie Hall* opened in April 1977, Diane Keaton would appear in another, altogether more sober role as the goodtime girl who falls foul of Richard Gere in *Looking for Mr Goodbar*.

When she came on to the stage in Los Angeles to accept her Academy Award for *Annie Hall* in early 1978, wearing her kooky, catch-all outfit, she seemed to embody the decade's casual, even flippant attitude to life. Allen, exhibiting even greater sang-froid, was tucked up in bed in New York as the awards were announced: Best Picture, Best Director, Best Actress and Best Original Screenplay. Besides, Mondays were – and still are – his chance to play the clarinet at Michael's Pub in Manhattan, and a trip to the West Coast could hardly outrank that in appeal.

Allen, like Coppola, has a shrewd eye for the promising newcomer (such as Sharon Stone as the 'Pretty Girl in the Train' in *Stardust Memories*). Two stars who made their first fleeting appearances in *Annie Hall* are Sigourney Weaver (just walking into a shot on the arm of an acquaintance of Alvy's, and not even showing us her full face) and Jeff Goldblum (or seen at a Beverly Hills party telling someone over the phone: 'Yeah, I forgot my mantra'). A slightly larger part goes to Christopher Walken, who had featured in films like *Next Stop Greenwich Village*, and who gives the character of Annie's younger brother a contained craziness as he talks of a dream in which he has an overwhelming desire to crash into an oncoming car.

Carol Kane, known for her roles in Bill Fruet's *Wedding in White* and Joan Micklin Silver's *Hester Street*, plays Alvy's first wife, and Janet Margolin, noted internationally in Leopoldo Torre Nilsson's *The Eavesdropper* (1966) before starring in Allen's debut feature *Take the Money and Run*, plays his second. Tony Roberts, a close friend of Allen's since they appeared on stage together in *Play It Again, Sam*, features as Alvy's buddy Rob, as he would in *Stardust Memories*. For the part of Annie's bourgeois mother Allen selected Colleen Dewhurst, who enthralled Broadway with her interpretations of so many Eugene O'Neill women, but never made an impact on the screen. Paul Simon, the songwriter and performer, glides through the latter portion of *Annie Hall* as the laid-back record producer lusting after Annie's talent – and her body. Allen credits Marshall Brickman with having suggested Simon for a part that fitted him like a glove.

Annie Hall almost runs 94 minutes, including titles and closing credits. The first cut was around two hours fifteen minutes, according to Marshall Brickman. 'What was excised in the editing process,' he recalls, 'was primarily material which, while funny (to the authors, anyhow), distracted from the emerging tale of Annie and Alvy and the pull their relationship seemed to be exerting on the story.'[11]

. . . .

Chaplin, so admired by Allen, drew many of his laughs at the expense of others – people like Henry Bergman who were so much bigger than he was, or those who were not smart enough to outwit Charlie in any given situation. Buster Keaton, the 'Great Stone Face', relied on his uncanny, even contortionist athletic ability to send audiences chuckling into the night. Laurel and Hardy were hilarious by virtue of their own overweening bickering and incompetence. Allen has acknowledged his link with the silent comedians. As a cabaret artist, 'I talked as myself. You know, insecurity in life, nervousness and insecurity towards women, inability in having good relationships, fear, cowardice – all the things that Charlie Chaplin or Buster Keaton played.' [12]

Yet only in the Jewish humour, the relentless verbal patter and sheer *chutzpah* of the Marx Brothers can we recognise an immediate kinship with Woody Allen. As Allen Eyles wrote in 1966 in his classic study of the team: 'They are the heroes of everyone who has suffered from other people's hypocrisy, pomposity, pedantry, and patronage. They settle for none of it. The Marxes assume that we join them on their comic crusade.' [13] Woody Allen could be described in much the same terms. The Jewish inferiority complex is 'outed' in a very early sequence of *Annie Hall*, as Alvy and his friend Rob walk along a Manhattan street and Alvy describes how he was 'baited' by an executive at NBC: 'Did you eat yet or what?' Alvy had asked a colleague. Back comes the response: ' "No, didchoo?" Not, did you, didchoo eat? *Jew?* No, not did you eat, but *jew* eat? *Jew?* You get it? *Jew* eat?' As Robert Benayoun has observed, 'Humour for Woody often is a Jewish prerogative.' [14]

Benny Green has written that 'While Groucho founded his super-lative delivery on a brutal aggression towards the deserving and undeserving alike, Allen affects a weak spineless persona to whom disasters accrue.' [15] Allen's sense of comedy too can be aggressive, but more often than not its force derives from a facility with words that belongs to the tradition of Groucho Marx and every Jewish stand-up who ever performed in the clubs and resort hotels of the 'Borscht circuit'. As many scenes in *Annie Hall* demonstrate, this type of humour depends on complicity with the audience. Like Groucho, Woody Allen will often flash an aside to the camera, although only he would dare to talk straight-faced into the lens for minutes on end.

Perhaps the true godfather of Allen's wit and wisdom is Mort Sahl, a Jewish comedian never immortalised on film but worshipped during the 50s for the effortless flow of humour he could produce in front of an audience. Allen has compared Sahl to Mark Twain, and consciously shares certain attributes with him: a naturalistic appearance on stage, an unforced delivery of patter, a love of digression, and what he himself has termed 'a stream of consciousness, [...] a kind of jazz rhythm'. [16] Even though Allen admires comics like Bob Hope, Danny Kaye, Sid Caesar and Jonathan Winters, he himself looks ill at ease in a tuxedo. That's why he is fond of quoting Groucho Marx's quip: 'I would never wanna belong to any club that would have someone like me for a member.'

THE ADORATION OF MANHATTAN

Woody Allen's adoration of New York City would reach its apotheosis in *Manhattan*, made two years after *Annie Hall*. Sitting at dawn beside the East River, he tells Diane Keaton's Mary that 'This is really a great city. I don't care what anybody says. It's just so – really a knockout, you know?' And in the offscreen prologue to *Manhattan*, his Isaac is heard essaying the opening lines of a new novel: 'He was too romantic about Manhattan as he was about everything else. He thrived on the hustle-bustle of the crowds and the traffic. [...] To him, New York meant beautiful women and street-smart guys who seemed to know all the angles. [...] New York was his town. And it always would be.' Shorn of violence, purged of grunginess, the city takes on a glistening aura of romance.

In *Annie Hall*, Allen's camera lingers on the Upper East Side, with its Madison Avenue boutiques, its Third Avenue movie theatres, its myriad restaurants, and its adamantine bridges – the Triboro, the 59th Street and the Brooklyn. Crime, or rather the fear of crime, does not trouble his characters; they walk the streets after dark, and they exchange comments with passers-by. Central Park seems as safe as the Elysian Fields. Mayhem in Allen's cinema remains confined to the past (*Bullets over Broadway*), to the realms of escapist melodrama (*Manhattan Murder Mystery*), or to betrayal on an intimate, concealed scale (*Crimes and Misdemeanours*).

In a society where money rather than birth dictates a person's class, Woody Allen and his friends on screen are unmistakably middle-class. Born in the shadow of the Coney Island roller-coaster in working-class Brooklyn, Alvy Singer escapes across the water to Manhattan and respectability, to a sophisticated metropolitan environment where Jews do not flaunt their folksiness. The need to make money is rarely an issue in Allen's cinema. The cash flows in sufficient quantities for his characters to have charge cards at Bloomingdales and to eat out at Elaine's. Hailing a cab, or playing indoor squash or tennis, is a spontaneous gesture born of long familiarity with the greenback. As we'll see later, all Allen's work is coloured by personal experience, and his characters either benefit from inherited wealth or earn well by virtue of their talent, as he himself has done from a quite early age.

Take financial exigencies out of the New York equation, and you're left with a world of Democrat intellectuals, Republican philistines, and a sprinkling of eccentric old ladies. As various scenes in *Annie Hall* make plain, Allen can stop to talk to strangers in the street in New York as though they were part of his own family. Manhattan consists of apartments, restaurants, sidewalks, as Allen himself once said.[17] Weekends in summer mean a trip to the little house in the Hamptons. Weekends in winter mean a visit to one of the city's museums, or a stroll in the Park.

Familiarity with this round has not, however, bred contempt in Woody Allen. He derives inspiration as well as energy from the glitter and the cacophony of New York, from the sheer compression of its topography, the fact that everything is within easy striking distance. Reactions are fast, bred of necessity. Everyone eats out, so that more than 25,000 restaurants flourish in the five boroughs, by day and by night.

2 0   Rob dons his helmet

Manhattan, shot in refulgent black-and-white, pays even greater homage than *Annie Hall* to the incandescent pulse of the city.

California, by comparison, is a seat of indolence, an amorphous state in which, to quote Alvy Singer on Los Angeles, 'the only cultural advantage is that you can make a right turn on a red light.' L.A. becomes the antithesis of New York, celebrating Christmas in bright sunshine, and obsessed with drugs, mantras, meetings, and the denial – literally – of Death. As Rob prepares to drive off after retrieving Alvy from jail in L.A., he dons a face helmet like something out of *The Hot Zone*. 'Keeps out the alpha rays,' he explains to Alvy. 'You don't get old.' Sun remains anathema to Alvy/Allen. In an early scene in *Annie Hall*, he tells Rob, 'Sun is bad for you. Everything our parents said was good is bad. Sun, milk, red meat, college...'

The food in California bewilders Alvy. 'I'm gonna have the alfalfa sprouts and, uh, a plate of mashed yeast,' he tells the squeaky-clean waitress as he waits for a rendezvous with Annie. So does the fixation with cars. Alvy, a native New Yorker accustomed to walking the streets and occasionally using cabs, finds himself behind the wheel of a rented car and finishes by crashing into several other vehicles in a parking lot, succumbing to a fiendish desire to relive his days at the Dodgems in Brooklyn.

Allen's vision of film culture in Manhattan is somewhat romantic; the number of classic and foreign films actually screening at any one time is pitiful by comparison with Paris. In *Annie Hall*, New York is the home of Bergman's *Face to Face* and Marcel Ophuls's *The Sorrow and the Pity*. Los Angeles, on the other hand, sports just one movie theatre, showing a double bill of *House of Exorcism* and *Messiah of Evil* (with the irony accentuated by the line 'To save us all from Satan's power' being sung offscreen in a radio programme of canned carols as Rob's sports car glides through the streets). Allen's native New Yorkers watch TV sparingly, and then for a purpose (for instance, Alvy's catching a Knicks' basketball game during a stultifying cocktail party). In Los Angeles, Rob becomes a producer for the small screen and takes glee in sharing with Alvy the cynical artifice of the medium, adding fake laughs to a pre-taped sitcom. Parties of any kind are anathema to Allen, and provoke his satiric scorn, but the inertia of the Beverly Hills gathering attended by Alvy and Rob in *Annie Hall* contrasts with the cultural pretentiousness of its Manhattan equivalent earlier when Robin and Alvy mingle with the literati.

In the twenty years since Allen shot his film, the balance of power in the entertainment world has tilted sharply towards the West Coast. One after another the decision-makers in film, television and music migrated to Los Angeles during the 80s, leaving Broadway and Madison Avenue as the only significant 'media' forces in New York. Rob's siren call in *Annie Hall* has proved seductive. Even the showbiz bible *Variety*, for decades associated with New York and the Great White Way, moved its headquarters to Hollywood in 1992. The crowds milling around the first-run multiplexes in Westwood or Brentwood today are probably just as informed and passionate about new movies as their counterparts in Manhattan.

Allen's disdain for California reaches back almost to his adolescence. In 1956, he spent several weeks in Los Angeles, appearing on the 'Colgate Show', and indeed married his first wife, Harlene, at the Hollywood Hawaiian Motel. 'Hollywood is a rural village that would bore you stiff in no time,' he wrote to a schoolfriend. 'Pray you, avoid it.'[18] In *Annie Hall*, Alvy reacts with shock to Annie's emigration to the West Coast: 'You want to live out here all year? It's like living in Munchkinland.'

From his earliest days as an independent film-maker (*Bananas, Take the Money and Run*), Woody Allen has insisted on shooting and editing his pictures in New York. Obviously, for a director so attuned to filming on location, he has honoured the occasional necessity of travelling to Los Angeles or to Italy, but he is relieved when circumstances allow him to remain in Manhattan. Most of his non-urban locations have been found within an hour's ride of New York City (such as the Pocantico Hills for *A Midsummer Night's Sex Comedy*). *Stardust Memories*, with its numerous locations, took some six months to shoot and reshoot, something that frustrated a director accustomed to controlling reality within the confines of a studio – or at least on the calmer streets of New York.

INSIDE 'ANNIE HALL'
. . . .

The opening scene of *Annie Hall* manages to acknowledge both Ingmar Bergman and the vaudeville tradition from which stand-up comedians like Woody Allen emerged. Seen in amiable if stark close-up, Alvy Singer starts talking to his audience, striking an acutely personal note from the very outset. He tells a couple of Jewish jokes and confesses his emotional problems: a mid-life crisis in the wake of his fortieth birthday (Allen himself had turned forty on 1 December 1975) and the break-up with Annie Hall.

Bergman pioneered this kind of 'confessional' close-up, in films like *Winter Light*, *Persona* and *Shame*, trapping his character in a tight frame, without benefit of make-up or the averted gaze. In *Annie Hall*, this scene telegraphs to the audience an instant table of references: we have the impression that this man has come on set wearing the same clothes as he does in everyday life; that he the director, Woody Allen, rather than Alvy Singer, is addressing us, taking us into his confidence, and turning to Chaplinesque advantage the familiarity of his face and gestures, his habitual garb of tweed jacket, plaid shirt and black-framed spectacles.

'I think the way you begin a film is important,' notes Allen. 'This comes probably from my cabaret training. It's important for the beginning and ending to have a special quality of some sort, a special theatrical quality, or something to arrest the audience immediately.'[19]

This avuncular tone persists as Alvy recalls his childhood in a small house in Brooklyn, reverberating beneath the gigantic Coney Island roller-coaster, to the discreet tones of Tommy Dorsey's music on

Alvy Singer (Woody Allen) talking to his audience

the soundtrack. Studious, arch and aggressive by turns, the young Alvy exhibits the latent characteristics of his adult personality. Allen takes gleeful revenge on his schooldays, mocking teachers and fellow pupils alike, and even materialising as his adult self to defend his having kissed a little playmate at the age of six ('I was just expressing a healthy sexual curiosity'). Indulging the daydream of returning in some magic time capsule to our childhood, Alvy asks his schoolmates where they are today. One boy runs a dress company. A little girl confesses that she is 'into leather', while another boy says, 'I used to be a heroin addict. Now I'm a methadone addict.' Allen told biographer Eric Lax that he 'hated the concept of school in every way because, emotionally, I wasn't prepared for readjustment.'[20] As he stands in line for *The Sorrow and the Pity*, though, he tells Annie that he's 'comparatively normal for a guy raised in Brooklyn'.

Already Allen has introduced some unexpected visual conceits, and the film continues to dart back and forth in time, conflating (but never confusing) memories and present-day experiences. The distinction between Woody Allen and Alvy Singer becomes increasingly difficult for the audience to sustain, and soon we abandon ourselves to the comfortable intimacy of the situation. When 'Alvy' appears on the Dick Cavett show, the videoscope image is undeniably 'real' to New Yorkers, who know that Allen himself really did feature on that selfsame show, and that he is referring to himself as much as to Alvy Singer when he declares that he became a comedian and then cracks the joke about being rejected by the Army and classified as '4-P – yes, in-in-in-in the event of war, I'm a hostage!'

Alvy's bosom pal Rob (played by Tony Roberts) is introduced in a deft and audacious shot that begins with voices off-screen and the camera staring the length of a quiet Manhattan sidewalk. Little by little, the figures of Alvy and Rob emerge from the distance, engaged in conversation. Alvy's agitated gait contrasts wittily with Rob's calm, complacent, upright walk. Alvy expostulates, Rob absorbs. Alvy's contention that he is the victim of some Jew-baiting conspiracy makes little impression on the WASPish Rob, who suggests that relocating to California will banish all such prejudicial afflictions. 'We move to sunny L.A.,' he intones. 'All of show business is out there, Max' – 'Max' being obviously a private joke between them. It so happens that Allen idolised Max Shulman, the writer, when he was young and toyed with the idea of

Alvy back in school

Alvy/Woody on the Dick Cavett show

Woody Allen and Tony Roberts on the sidewalk in Manhattan

adopting Max as his first name when, in 1952, he decided to relinquish his real name of Allen Konigsberg in favour of something simpler and more appropriate to a comedian.

Another nod to Bergman occurs in the ensuing sequence, as Alvy waits on Second Avenue for Annie to arrive at the Beekman cinema. Posters for *Face to Face* (released in 1976) dominate the background of several shots, and while an obnoxious stranger keeps pestering Alvy about his appearances on TV, Alvy mutters an aside for the benefit of the audience – 'I need a large polo mallet' – invoking the imagery of Chaplin's silent comedy which Allen so adores. The man's bumptious request for an autograph anticipates a female fan's demand in *Stardust Memories* that Allen should sign her left breast.

With the arrival of Diane Keaton's Annie by cab, the references to 70s 'civilisation' proliferate (see Glossary). Alvy tells her that he has been standing with the cast of *The Godfather*, and in his next line refers to his unwelcome fans as 'two guys named Cheech'. He accuses her of being in a bad mood because of her period. 'Jesus, every time anything out of the ordinary happens, you think that I'm getting my period!' exclaims Annie. The exchange recurs later in the film, and it's a homage to Bergman's *Scenes from a Marriage*, released in the United States in 1974. Erland Josephson chides Liv Ullmann in almost identical fashion, and her reply echoes Annie's: 'Even if my period is due on Monday, that's not necessarily why I feel like blowing my top!' Allen's relationships resemble Bergman's in their unpredictable changes of mood, switching from childish exhilaration one moment to vindictive squabbling the next.

Exasperated at the thought of entering the movie two minutes after it has begun (even though Annie assures him that they'll only miss the titles – and they're in Swedish), Alvy drags his date across to the Upper West Side to another film buff's mecca, The New Yorker.

Time and again in his films, Allen shows a knack of creating hilarious situations in the very thick of his narrative, milking them for all they're worth – and not a second more – before passing to the next stage in a relationship. Now in the line at the New Yorker, Alvy and Annie make small-talk and when she outrages him by mentioning 'my sexual problem', he says earnestly, 'Wasn't that a novel by Henry James? A sequel to *The Turn of the Screw?*' Behind them, an intellectual pontificates to his companion about Fellini's indulgence as a film-maker. Alvy listens with mounting frustration, and then suddenly leaves the line and comes forward to address the camera: 'What do you do when you get stuck in a movie line with a guy like this behind you?'

This gimmick may lose its effect with repetition, but Allen caps it with a *coup de théâtre* that only he among contemporary comedians could engineer with such aplomb. As the objectionable academic type boasts that he teaches the work of Marshall McLuhan in classes at Columbia University, Alvy announces that he happens to have Mr McLuhan right there. And from behind a signboard in the lobby of the theatre a distinguished, if rather bemused, McLuhan actually appears. Such magical effects occur also in *Play It Again, Sam*, *The Purple Rose of Cairo*, *Oedipus Wrecks* and other Allen works, as Diane Jacobs has pointed out.[21] Allen had asked Federico Fellini to 'appear' in this scene, 'because it would be more natural if people were standing in line talking about movies, that they would be talking about Fellini.'[22] But the Italian maestro disliked travelling, and could not come to the US for shooting.

In putting down Alvy's tormentor, McLuhan satirises himself with the impeccable line, 'You know nothing of my work; you mean, my whole fallacy is wrong.' The casual misuse of words belongs to the essence of Allen's wit and to his years of training as a stand-up comedian. In a later scene, Alvy refers to a magazine called *Dysentery*. His wife Robin corrects him with a patronising look: '*Commentary*.' But Alvy persists: 'Oh really, I heard that *Commentary* and *Dissent* had merged to form *Dysentery*.' Such quips sparkle in the pages of Allen's early routines, such as 'The Great Renaldo', and in the *New Yorker* items collected in the volume *Without Feathers* (1975). *Commentary* had already been referred to in Allen's earlier feature, *Bananas*.

Each flashback in *Annie Hall* illustrates some watershed or vignette in Alvy and Annie's life, and revives the savour of a certain period. As a chance remark by Annie triggers a sequence involving Alvy meeting his first wife Allison at a political rally for Adlai Stevenson, we can deduce from the dialogue that it must be early 1960 and the final months of the Eisenhower administration (or perhaps even 1956, when Stevenson actually won the Democratic nomination for a second time). Allison wears an 'Adlai' button, and Alvy, shrewdly assessing the needs of the moment, does his thing on stage and makes a joke at Eisenhower's expense. Much later in the film, when Alvy and Annie are splitting up, they sift through a box full of buttons: 'Impeach Nixon', 'Impeach Johnson', 'Impeach Eisenhower'.

In a smooth, almost subliminal transition, Alvy and Allison are discovered in bed. Our first assumption is that they've only just met. But here they are arguing about the Kennedy assassination, several years after the night of the Stevenson rally, and the relationship has run its course. Alvy, the archetypal conspiracy theorist, exasperates Allison, who tells him with withering resignation that she loves 'being reduced to a cultural stereotype'. Allen's genius extrapolates from the general to the particular, compressing the debate of a generation into a brief bedroom scene, just as the fashionable late 60s–early 70s obsession with mysticism fuels the later sequence involving Alvy and his girlfriend from *Rolling Stone*.

Allen's films concern themselves with emotional politics, not with political life. Over the years, the Democrats have won most elections in New York City, and Allen fits the slightly left-of-centre profile of the typical Manhattan Democrat. Just before shooting *Annie Hall*, he had taken a leading role in Martin Ritt's *The Front*, which revived the days of Senator McCarthy and the Hollywood blacklist. But there is no more evidence of political 'commitment' in Allen's cinema than there is in Bergman's or Truffaut's or Fellini's. His sympathetic characters all tend towards the offbeat profession and an interest in the arts. The three

Allison (Carol Kane) with her 'Adlai' button

giants of the TV talkshow in the early 70s were Johnny Carson, David Frost and Dick Cavett. Although he sometimes hosted the Johnny Carson show, Allen's kinship lay with the liberal, intellectual, faintly aloof Cavett, and not just because over the years they had become friends in real life.

Alvy may be surrounded by stereotypes, but Allen the director delights in puncturing their self-esteem. *Annie Hall* features a splendid gallery of such characters: Allison the activist, Robin the po-faced bluestocking, Pam the *Rolling Stone* reporter, Tony the record producer...

In another aside to the camera, Alvy confesses his inability to stay with someone like Allison, even though she is 'real ... beautiful ... intelligent', and he suspects that once again he may be like Groucho Marx in not wanting to belong to any club that would have him as a member. Allen had spoken directly to the camera in earlier films, and most subtly in *Love and Death*. Alvy's tendency to digress in moments when concentration is required will prove his undoing. Bedroom sex in Allen's films rarely reaches a satisfactory climax, because the comedian's mind flits to some offscreen obsession at the expense of tenderness and persistence.

'Talk to him, you speak shellfish!'

Brisk transitions contribute to the effervescent durability of *Annie Hall*. From Alvy's resigned acceptance of his break-up with Allison, we cut to a shot of a house in the Hamptons, where Alvy and Annie work each other into a lather in their clumsy pursuit of lobsters on the kitchen floor. 'Talk to him, you speak shellfish!' exclaims Alvy at one point. According to Eric Lax, this was the first scene shot for the film, 'and neither Woody nor Diane was acting. Their laughter was completely spontaneous and it gives the scene a vitality that cannot be planned.'[23] Willis's hand-held camera seems to dart around the cramped space of the kitchen in a single take, and the hilarious scene prefigures one later in the film when Alvy chases a spider in Annie's bathroom.

As the lovers stroll along the Long Island shore at dusk, Alvy prompts Annie to recall her earlier relationships too. First up is Dennis, kissing Annie in front of a poster of John Huston's *The Misfits*, situating the scene around 1961. Offscreen, Alvy continues talking to Annie in the present, imagining her as looking like 'the wife of an astronaut' (not far wrong, to judge by the women's hairdos in both *The Right Stuff* and *Apollo 13*). A more serious and pretentious suitor is Jerry, 'the actor', bearded like the pard and full of bullshit as he tells a susceptible Annie that he yearns to die 'torn apart by wild animals,' triggering Alvy's

3 0   Alvy and Annie watch Annie with Jerry

offscreen response, 'Heavy! Eaten by some squirrels.' The notion of merging past and present in a single scene appeals to Allen. He resorts to it later in *Annie Hall*, when Rob, Annie and Alvy observe the goings-on in the Singer household circa 1945; and in *The Purple Rose of Cairo* the concept underscores the entire film.

Now comes a first hearing of 'La-di-da', the expression that Annie utters with her inimitable giggle at various junctures, implying not so much derision as self-deprecation. Diane Keaton made this a trademark for her personality, with its overtones of fecklessness and discombobulation (to quote a favourite word of one of the 70s quintessential icons, Henry Kissinger). 'If anyone had ever told me that I'd be taking out a girl who used expressions like "la-di-da",' muses Alvy, suggesting the contrast between Annie's air-headed out-of-town personality and the pencil-sharp, ineffably humourless 'sophistication' of Alvy's two Manhattan wives, Allison and Robin. Annie provides him with an antidote to the structured artifice of his New York existence.

Robin, her hair in a severe bun and a patronising stare behind her large spectacles, emerges in the next flashback. She squires Alvy round a publisher's party, fending off his puns and jokes and pointing out the Great and the Good with relish while Alvy moans about wanting to see the Knicks on television. Allen has a passion for basketball in general, and for the Knicks in particular. If, while shooting a film, he cannot attend a Knicks' home game, he'll let members of his crew use his four courtside seats.[24] In *Annie Hall*, Robin's disdain for the sport ('What's so fascinating about a group of pituitary cases trying to stuff a ball through a hoop?') condemns her as an intellectual who 'can be absolutely brilliant and have no idea what's going on.'

If the archetypal Allen personality needs a shrink to survive in everyday life, then his bedroom encounters demand drugs of one kind or another for there to be any hope of success. Robin complains about the noise of a passing siren as she is about to climax in Alvy's arms, and then calls for her Valium, just as Annie feels the need to smoke pot.

Like onion skins, one flashback peels back to reveal another. Alvy's bed scene with Robin cuts to a Manhattan tennis club, where Alvy and his friend Rob will meet Annie Hall for the first time. Before they reach the court, Alvy again inveighs against the rabid anti-Semitism of all and sundry. 'Don't you see,' he tells an uninterested Rob, 'The rest of the country looks upon New York like we're, we're left-wing Communist,

Jewish, homosexual pornographers. I think of us that way, sometimes, and I live here.'

Annie is introduced on court, and covers her embarrassment with a cascade of exclamations, such as 'Egads!' and 'Holy Gods!' This continues as she meets Alvy outside the locker rooms, and an elaborate ballet of gestures ensues as the two of them offer each other a lift. She's going downtown, he uptown, then she changes her mind with a giggle and they head north in her open-roofed Volkswagen. It's an alarming ride that must remind Alvy of the chase scene in *The French Connection*, even if he does elicit the information that Annie comes from Chippewa Falls, Wisconsin (Keaton herself was born in Los Angeles).[26] From his response, it's clear that Alvy regards anything west of the Hudson as galactic in its remoteness.

But once safely landed on the sidewalk after this hair-raising journey, Alvy launches into what amounts to a stuttering paean of praise for all that the kooky Annie represents. 'You're a wonderful tennis player... and the worst driver I've ever seen in my life ... and I love what you're wearing', referring to her tie and, by implication, the whole caboodle: waistcoat, men's shirt, baggy chinos, floppy hat.

Their courtship proceeds in a ballet of fidgets and nods, and a

3 2   'I love what you're wearing' – Annie's kooky outfit

partsong of questions, counter-questions, non-sequiturs and nervous apologies. She absorbs the fact that Alvy has been seeing an analyst for fifteen years. Woody Allen himself has been visiting doctors throughout his life, and 'likens the process to hitting with a tennis pro once a week: a useful exercise.'[25] Annie tells her new-found friend that he's what her grandmother would call 'a real Jew'. 'Grammy Hall' hates Jews and thinks they just make money, and this fearsome creature will live up to her reputation in a subsequent scene at the Hall family residence.

Experimenting again, Allen now offers a kind of dialectical dialogue: as Annie and Alvy chat vacuously about photography, their real thoughts pop up in subtitle form at the foot of the screen, each wondering if the relationship has a chance of evolving. A typical exchange runs like this:

> ANNIE: Aesthetic criteria? You mean, whether it's a good photo or not? (Subtitle: *I'm not smart enough for him. Hang in there.*)
> ALVY: The medium enters in as a condition of the art form itself. That's — (Subtitle: *I don't know what I'm saying. She senses I'm shallow.*)

At last they find a common factor that truly unites them in mutual sympathy. A timid Annie is about to sing for the first time in a nightclub. 'I know exactly what's that like,' says Alvy in an attempt to reassure her. Before each appearance as a stand-up comedian, Allen was always jelly-kneed, although once he had launched into his routine the stage-fright vanished. Some of his own early experiences in Jewish social clubs must be reflected in the sequence showing Annie's debut as a singer. The camera stares at her with relentless concentration from different angles as she churns out an iffy rendition of 'It Had to Be You', to the accompaniment of breaking crockery, a shrilling phone, a humming mike, and customers chattering to each other oblivious of Annie and her well-meaning incompetence.

This section of the film proves the most engaging, with each conversation bringing the lovers closer together, despite their ethnic differences (Alvy grimaces with wry amusement as Annie orders a pastrami on white bread with mayonnaise and lettuce and tomato). Sex is heaven: 'As Balzac said, "There goes another novel." Jesus, you were great,' sighs Alvy as they lie in bed together. Browsing in a bookshop, he introduces her to Ernest Becker's *The Denial of Death* and Jacques Choron's *Death and Western Thought*, as passionately as she had defended Sylvia Plath's poems in her apartment.

Seated on a bench in Central Park, they make frivolous comments about passers-by, with Alvy invoking Truman Capote, the Mafia and the typical habitués of Miami or Fire Island. Later, strolling beneath the 59th Street Bridge, Alvy squeezes her arm affectionately and commends her sex appeal – 'You're polymorphously perverse […] You're exceptional in bed because you get pleasure in every part of your body when I touch you.'

Yet a subtext of doubt persists in the face of all Alvy's wooing. Annie's enigmatic smile disguises a reluctance to endorse Alvy's view of their relationship, 'I really like you' falling significantly short of 'I love you'. The seeds of their break-up are already discernible even in this most romantic of scenes (one that is replicated almost exactly in *Manhattan*).

Alvy, too, has misgivings, especially when Annie moves into his apartment with all her goods and chattels. He puts the issue succinctly when he declares, 'We live together, we sleep together, we eat together. Jesus, you don't want it to be like we're married, do you?' In a memorable, Bergmanesque line in *A Midsummer Night's Sex Comedy*, the Tony Roberts character, reminiscent of Gunnar Björnstrand in *Smiles of a Summer Night*, declares that 'marriage is the death of hope.'

An exhilarating snatch from Mozart's Jupiter Symphony backs another excursion to Long Island, and yet another bedroom scene that begins on a promising note and ends in the couple going through the motions of love-making, she seeking inspiration from a joint, and he wearing his socks and producing an 'erotic artefact' – a red lightbulb – he's brought from the city. Just as Allen earlier used subtitles to communicate real thoughts, so here he permits a bored Annie to rise from herself in the bed and sit and watch her conversation with Alvy, rather as David Holm emerges from his body in Sjöström's *The Phantom Carriage*. The trick in this conceit lies in Alvy talking as though both he and Annie know that her alter ego is replying from a chair on the other side of the room. 'Oh, you have my body,' says Annie, and Alvy's reply – 'That's no good, I want the whole thing' – demonstrates that for him possession is nine-tenths of love, as it is of the law.

. . . .

The film stumbles only when Woody Allen digresses from the essential relationship with Annie. The scenes in Alvy's manager's office, and then on stage at the University of Wisconsin, probably come full-blown from Allen's own past. For some years he provided established comedians with jokes for their columns and shows. But there's a certain condescension in Allen's treatment of the brash comedian (Johnny Haymer, for whom Allen did provide material in his early days) who shows off his less than scintillating routine to a polite Alvy and his cigar-chomping agent (played by Bernie Styles, although it could have been either Jack Rollins or Charlie Joffe, Allen's real-life agents and themselves inveterate cigar-smokers). It's a smidgin self-indulgent because we then segue into Alvy's own flawless performance before a packed auditorium of enthusiastic students. Every joke hits the button, and Alvy finds himself surrounded by autograph hunters after the show. 'I'm starting to get more of your references too,' says Annie, who regards him with increased admiration after such a triumph at her alma mater.

In terms of narrative, the transition works well because Alvy has the excuse to meet Annie's Midwestern family the following day. Few directors in America can film a domestic meal as skilfully as Woody

A ghostly Annie watches herself with Alvy

Allen. Apart from *Husbands and Wives*, where Carlo Di Palma's camera zips around impatiently, such scenes benefit from careful planning on the director's part (for example, the Thanksgiving dinner in *Hannah and Her Sisters*). Allen told the *New York Times* in 1977 that he recalled having Thanksgiving dinner with one of Diane Keaton's grandmothers: 'A beautiful American family. I felt I was an alien or exotic object to them, a nervous, anxiety-ridden, suspicious, wise-cracking kind of strange bird. After dinner, all these grammies sat around playing poker... My family would've been exchanging gunfire.'[27]

The Jewish theme emerges again, with a vengeance. As Alvy struggles on Easter Sunday to masticate the ham he knows he should never be eating, the bigoted old granny gives him a malevolent stare, changing him in her mind's eye to an Orthodox Jew complete with black hat, beard and tresses. Annie's mother mentions the fact that he's been seeing a psychiatrist for fifteen years. 'Yes, I'm making excellent progress,' replies Alvy politely. 'Pretty soon when I lie down on his couch, I won't have to wear the lobster bib.' Nobody laughs.

Alvy soon turns to the camera and compares this demure, utterly repellent family with his own raucous parents in Brooklyn. The split-screen effect is amusing if not revolutionary (and is used by Allen again

3 6   Alvy imagined as an Orthodox Jew

later in *Annie Hall* as well as in films like *Stardust Memories*), but the originality of the sequence stems from the families' actually addressing each other across the divided screen. Mom Hall asks Mrs Singer how they plan to spend the holidays, and is flummoxed by the concept of atoning for one's sins by fasting. 'What sins?' she queries. 'I don't understand.' Back comes the retort from Alvy's pa: 'Tell you the truth, neither do we.' As in the best moments of Allen's cinema, a verbal wisecrack meets a visual invention.

A European audience might, on hearing the anti-Jewish expletives splattered throughout Martin Scorsese's *Casino*, be appalled. Not so the American filmgoer. Lay Jews in the United States can tolerate remarks about their ethnic origin much more equably than their counterparts in, say, Britain or France, and Jewish humour raises laughter in clubs and resort hotels down a wide swathe of the Eastern seaboard. As Robert Benayoun has remarked, Woody Allen 'illustrates the royal progress of the American comic who evolved out of the reception centres of Ellis Island and then scattered through the suburbs of Brooklyn and the "Jewish Alps" (Catskills, Adirondacks).'[28] Nearly all the comedians Allen admires stem from this Jewish behavioural tradition: Charlie Chaplin, the Marx Brothers, George S. Kaufman, Mort Sahl, Sid Caesar, Milton Berle, S. J. Perelman. Being Jewish did not make much impact on Allen as a youngster, but although he has never embraced the orthodox dogma of Judaism, he has become increasingly preoccupied with questions of morality and metaphysics in his 'serious' pictures like *Interiors*, *Another Woman* and *Crimes and Misdemeanours*.

Two short scenes involving Annie's younger brother, Duane, who sounds like a potential psychotic, do little to flesh out the main theme. In hindsight, however, the close-up of Alvy through a rain-strewn windscreen on the way to the airport can be viewed as metaphorically, not literally, a watershed. Shaken by his ham-packed Easter Sunday encounter with the Halls, Alvy fears both for his life at the hands of Duane behind the wheel and for the future of his relationship with a goy whose family regards him as something from outer space.

Sure enough, the next sequence monitors Alvy's first suspicions of infidelity. Annie has been seeing her college professor, who teaches an adult education class in 'Existential Motifs in Russian Literature', and Alvy surprises her in the street after school. When she puts him down for referring to masturbation, Alvy responds with one of the film's funniest lines: 'Hey, don't knock masturbation. It's sex with someone I love!' Their argument concludes on an ominous note, with Annie reminding Alvy that he had shied away from making a real commitment because she's insufficiently 'smart'. The same gibe surfaces at the end of the following sequence, as Annie describes her maiden encounter with a shrink: 'I told her about I didn't think you'd ever really take me seriously, because you don't think that I'm smart enough.'

This also points to a Pygmalion and Galatea element in the relationship, as there has been in the real-life friendship between Woody Allen and Diane Keaton. Alvy longs to possess Annie, to shape her in his image. He introduces her to books 'about Death', recommends her to undergo analysis, and urges her to take adult education courses. The myth goes awry for Alvy because he cannot bring himself to marry his model and, like most latterday Galateas, Annie eludes his clutches and transcends his sphere of influence.

Exasperated by Annie's attraction to her professor, Alvy sees her noisily into a taxi and then engages in a spot of vox pop to endorse his views. He asks a succession of surprised pedestrians for their views on love, sex and the whole damned thing. 'You look like a really happy couple,' he says to a bland, amiable man and woman strolling along the street. 'How do you account for it?'

'Er, I'm very shallow and empty and I have no ideas and nothing interesting to say,' replies the girl.

'And I'm exactly the same way,' chimes her partner.

Allen then wrong-foots his own audience by invoking Walt Disney's *Snow White and the Seven Dwarfs*, and the screen offers us an animated pastiche (created by Chris Ishii) of a scene from the film, with the Wicked Queen looking unmistakably like Annie. 'Everyone fell in love with Snow White,' intones Alvy, recalling his childhood. 'I immediately fell for the Wicked Queen.' Rob enters the tableau too, and starts telling Alvy to forget about Annie and take his pick of any number of women, one of whom is a reporter with *Rolling Stone*.

Shelley Duvall, discovered by Robert Altman in the early 70s, plays Pam, the deadpan, spaced-out journalist, an archetype of the decade's obsession with all things spurious and spiritual. After testing his physical resources in bed ('I'm starting to get some feeling back in my jaw now,' yawns Alvy), she declares that sex with him is a 'Kafkaesque experience – I mean that as a compliment.' Allen lies back on a single

Alvy with the Wicked Queen

Shelly Duvall as Pam

pillow, exhausted, while Pam sits propped up smoking a cigarette. She is the dominant figure, like the Wicked Queen, who hovers above a tiny, big-headed Alvy in the cartoon sequence. Few comedians apart from Danny De Vito have made such capital from their shortness of stature as Woody Allen does, and almost invariably during erotic scenes. Shelley Duvall's stork-like presence is akin to Charlotte Rampling's in *Stardust Memories*, or Meryl Streep's in *Manhattan*.

A phone call from Annie interrupts this idyll, and opens the last truly intimate and congenial phase in the relationship with Alvy. She has found a spider in her apartment, and summons Alvy to despatch it. But Alvy's arachnophobia matches his fear of lobsters, and he needs a tennis racket to deal with the invader, smashing in the process various items in Annie's cramped bathroom.[29] Of course the real reason for Annie's call is her woman's instinctive guesstimate that he has been sleeping with someone else. Soon they are lovey-dovey in bed again, and resolving never to part. They speed out of town with Rob for the weekend, and eavesdrop on a flashback to Alvy's youth, with his parents arguing over the fate of a cleaning lady, and then his cousin Herbie returning after World War II, and plain, rather lumpen aunt Tessie ('She's the life of the ghetto, no doubt,' smiles Alvy).

These autobiographical memories mean a lot to Allen. They evoke a childhood during which the concept of family was sovereign. Throughout his adult life Allen has recoiled from that image, not fathering a child until the age of fifty and preferring always a solitary bachelor existence in his East Side penthouse, even during his halcyon days with Mia Farrow, who lived on the other side of the park with her numerous offspring. The Brooklyn boyhood he describes in *Annie Hall*, however, provides also the source of his wit and wisdom, his streetwise savvy that allows him to flourish in New York's frenetic round.

Alvy emphasises both the naughty and the sensitive sides of his nature when he gives Annie her birthday presents: some black lingerie that shocks her, and a watch that she has coveted for ages. And immediately after this, Allen the director, Allen the ex-lover, sends a final 'visual valentine'[30] to Diane Keaton. For more than two minutes he films her in Bergmanesque close-up, singing 'Seems Like Old Times' in a nightclub. The shot embodies all Alvy's feelings of affection for Annie, while Annie's confident rendition of the song contrasts with her misbegotten stab at 'It Had to Be You' earlier in the film.

Diane Keaton sings in the nightclub

Annie and Alvy talking to their psychiatrists

As they stand drinking at the bar afterwards, a record producer, Tony Lacey, makes a suave appearance with his entourage. He wants Annie and Alvy to come back to their hotel to chat with Jack Nicholson and Anjelica Huston ('Just relax, just be very mellow'), but Alvy's antennae go up and he pleads a previous engagement. Justifying his grouchiness, he tells Annie later, 'If I get too mellow, I ripen and then rot...'

Allen uses split-screen once more to show Annie and Alvy talking to their respective psychiatrists, raising a laugh as each refers to their sexual rhythm and then to the expense of the consultations. 'I thought it was an interesting thing how two people report the same phenomenon differently,' Allen has said. 'I thought the point was most theatrically made that way.' [31]

The prospect of a visit to California emerges in the next scene, as Annie and Alvy josh with some friends who are snorting coke. Annie reproaches her lover: 'You never want to try anything new, Alvy,' she says, articulating what might be an underlying refrain for the film. Allen times the scene's big gag to perfection, sneezing a pile of white powder into oblivion right after hearing that it costs around $2,000 an ounce.

So to southern California, that state of mind so mocked by Woody Allen in so many of his plays and films. The obsession with health and cleanliness, with sunshine and sobriety, runs counter to the director's beloved New York. Christmas week in Manhattan is something Alvy hates to miss; in Los Angeles, Santa Claus and a horse-drawn sleigh stand immaculate on a Beverly Hills lawn, and the residential architecture is a mishmash – 'Spanish, next to Tudor, next to Japanese,' muses Alvy, as his friend Rob drives him and Annie through the spotless streets to the accompaniment of Christmas carols on the radio. 'It's clean 'cos they don't throw away their garbage. They keep it and make it into television shows,' whines Alvy.

At a Beverly Hills party, where it becomes obvious that Annie is falling under the spell of Tony Lacey, the record producer, Allen's dialogue slices and dices the West Coast affectation without mercy. 'Right now it's only a notion,' says one guy, 'but I think I can get money to turn it into a concept, and later turn it into an idea.'

Annie finds herself responding to the allure of L.A. more than Alvy ever could. 'That was fun,' she muses to herself on the plane back to New York, 'I don't think California is bad at all. It's a drag coming home.' She and Alvy come to the conclusion, side by side in First Class,

On the plane back to New York: 'I think what we have on our hands is a dead shark.' 43

that their romance has failed. 'A relationship is like a shark,' says Alvy. 'It has to constantly move forward or it dies. And I think what we have on our hands is a dead shark.' Diane Jacobs detects a marked distinction between *Annie Hall* and romantic comedies of earlier decades. The couple's problems 'would have been confronted and elaborated upon in crisis after crisis in the film's first hour and then have vanished or been made to seem trivial in light of the couple's shared affection, experience, and a far more troubling prospect of separation.'[32]

Book by book, souvenir by souvenir, hang-up by hang-up, Alvy and Annie dismantle their shared past. As Alvy waits outside a Third Avenue cinema, an acquaintance (with the then unknown Sigourney Weaver on his arm) announces that Annie is living in California with Tony Lacey. Trying to date other women has proved depressing for Alvy, and it's illustrated with a pang of regret in a 'remake' of the lobsters-in-the-kitchen sequence. Alvy's girlfriend this time is young and serious and rather dumb, and fails to appreciate his quips.

In a final, impulsive effort to retrieve his happiness, Alvy flies out to L.A., hires a car, and arranges to meet Annie at an outdoor restaurant. But as they argue across the table, and Annie accuses him of being unable to enjoy life, the passion and zany self-confidence that illuminate Alvy's personality in New York seem to fade in the sunshine of California.

Like Strindberg, who hissed at his critics that he would see them in his next play, Alvy writes a drama that, when rehearsed in Manhattan, contains most of the same lines as he and Annie exchange at the health restaurant on Sunset Boulevard. Alvy turns to the camera with a shrug: 'What do you want? – It was my first play. You know how you're always trying to get things to come out perfect in art, 'cos it's real difficult in life.' He recalls their last real encounter, with Annie and her new partner (played by Walter Bernstein, screenwriter for *The Front*) about to see Ophuls's *The Sorrow and the Pity*. The documentary, which in its two earlier appearances in *Annie Hall* has underlined the Jewish theme, now stares from the marquee like some poignant title for the dying fall of Alvy's romance.

After the lovers have a final, friendly lunch, Allen ushers in a reprise of Annie's singing 'Seems Like Old Times', to the accompaniment of a montage of flashbacks, brief snatches of happiness from the scrap-book of their life. Then Alvy and Annie say their farewells at the corner opposite Lincoln Center, while offscreen Alvy tells the joke about the man who goes to a psychiatrist because his brother thinks he's a chicken.

'Well,' says the doctor, 'why don't you turn him in?'

'I would,' says the guy, 'but I need the eggs', an irrefutable comment that for Allen and Alvy alike sums up the absurdity of relationships and the craving we all have for them. So the film concludes in the tone of its introduction, with Alvy the raconteur speaking candidly to his audience. Now, however, there is a dialectic between Alvy's offscreen résumé and the rather desolate image of him walking in the streets on the Upper West Side, a part of the topography he adores though he is without any question a lonely individual.

Talking to Stig Björkman, Allen explained that this monologue was not in the screenplay, but rather in the original murder mystery script which became *Annie Hall*. 'Since all I had was the street and the little café, [it seemed right] to let the two of them vanish and just let the street life flow on. It was some instinctive sense that I had. I felt that it sucked the audience up and gave an intensified feeling. And later, when I saw it with the music [Keaton singing 'Seems Like Old Times'], it seemed correct, so I left it that way.'[33]

Alvy and Annie say their farewells

VISUAL INVENTION

The outrageous, often prodigious risk-taking achieved by Woody Allen in *Everything You Wanted to Know About Sex... But Were Afraid to Ask* established him as an experimental film-maker. The imaginative use of locations in *Love and Death* confirmed that talent, and, for Diane Jacobs, '*Annie Hall* is Allen's most eclectic and innovative film: exploiting split-screen, animation, instant replay, and visual stream-of-consciousness devices, introducing a subtitled courtship interlude and several scenes of splintered realism where Alvy leaves the confines of plot to mull over events with his audience.'[34]

The underlying seriousness of the dilemmas posed in *Annie Hall* does not deter Allen from scattering his curlicues of visual invention throughout the film. Many owe a debt to the freewheeling antics pioneered by Godard and Lester during the 60s. During an early flashback to his childhood, for example, Alvy visits Coney Island and a blonde in a flame-orange dress dashes past, breaking stride to blow a kiss at the camera, like Anna Karina in *Une femme est une femme*. Others recall the early Bergman. In *Summer Interlude*, the characters drawn by Henrik and Marie on a scratch pad suddenly come to animated life, making a point about their relationship. Alvy Singer recalls his fondness for the Wicked Queen in *Snow White and the Seven Dwarfs*, and without warning the screen is filled with a brief pastiche of the Disney cartoon.

Addressing the camera, as though talking to a nightclub audience, came easily to Allen, who had spent his formative years as a stand-up comedian. It required more courage to let his characters, and not just Alvy, talk *outside* the screen, and for this Allen credits cinematographer Gordon Willis. By allowing Alvy to talk both within and beyond the shot of Annie reading in bed in his apartment, for instance, Allen expands the frame of reference, much as Antonioni did in *L'Avventura* when he kept his camera fixed on a wall or a square long after the characters had moved out of frame. During the weekend out on Long Island, Allen uses one prolonged, 'empty' tracking shot looking out across the sea at sunset, while off screen we hear Alvy and Annie talking to each other.

Allen takes time travel to a new level in several scenes in *Annie Hall*, allowing his characters to wander without preamble into some incident from the past, much as Anita Björk recalls her own childhood in Sjöberg's film of *Miss Julie*. Alvy can pop up in his old Brooklyn primary school and, when the teacher reprimands him for kissing a little girl in class, 'adult' Alvy can retort that he was just expressing a healthy sexual curiosity; Alvy, Rob and Annie can giggle at the domestic banter of Alvy's parents in the 40s; Alvy can stand by and watch Annie's insufferable college boyfriend going down on his knees to place her foot on his heart.

There are two sequences that rely on the split screen for their laughs and their social comment. The first permits the Halls and the Singers to talk to each other on Easter Sunday across a yawning ethnic divide, while the imagery sketches the essential differences between them – the Singers rambunctious and informal, the Halls sober and aloof. In the second, Alvy and Annie are seen talking to their respective shrinks. Not only the lines are funny, but also the contrasting tableaux – Alvy lying full-length on a leather couch in a panelled consulting room, with his psychiatrist looking away from him with as much detachment as a fellow member in a London club reading-room; and Annie in a Charles Eames-type armchair enveloped by white, clinical walls and functional furnishings.

Annie Hall contains far fewer shots than the average American feature film, although Allen breaks up his extended shots with more orthodox cutting back and forth in conversation pieces, so that the forward momentum of the film is sustained. Many of his shots last for over a minute, and some for much longer (Annie's rendition of 'Seems Like Old Times' in the nightclub lasts two minutes and twenty-five seconds – just one close-up punctuated by a brief shot from the back of the club).

The long take performs different functions in *Annie Hall*. The camera stands rooted to the spot for more than a minute as the college professor sounds off about Fellini and Marshall McLuhan in the lobby of the New Yorker, but it performs a 360 degree movement in the bedroom scene involving Allison and Alvy; this one minute forty seconds shot is achieved with self-effacing skill, in part because all the emphasis falls on the dialogue. This scene comes right before a one minute eighteen seconds shot in the kitchen on Long Island, as Alvy and Annie hunt for lobsters and the camera has to bob and weave to accommodate their antics.

Although he prefers real locations, Allen's facility for blocking shots inside apartments gives *Annie Hall* its fluidity even during potentially stagey dialogue sequences. When Alvy first visits Annie's small apartment, the shot lasts ninety seconds and passes through doorways and cramped rooms. And when he returns to the apartment many moons later, to rescue Annie from the threat of a huge black spider, the shot extends for seventy-two seconds.

The tracking shots in the streets of Manhattan are planned with equal care. The argument between Alvy and Annie over her college professor lasts for seventy seconds without a break, as the camera glides alongside them in medium close-up. In an interesting variation on the tracking shot, Allen films Alvy and Rob walking towards us engrossed in conversation. Only after almost a minute, as they come into close range, does the camera start to pull back and glide alongside them for another spell until the scene ends. These long exterior takes ensure that the characters, often viewed from across a street, blend into their urban surroundings. They talk alongside each other, rather than face to face or head to head.

Rarely does Allen depend on a cut to produce a laugh. One of his funniest transitions, though, contrasts Alvy extolling the virtues of adult education to Annie in his apartment with his denouncing its flaws immediately afterwards as he helps Annie into a cab.

Bergman's *Persona*, one of Allen's favourite films, has the audacity to repeat a long monologue by Bibi Andersson word for word, from a different angle. In the final throes of *Annie Hall*, we hear two young actors rehearsing a play by Alvy; they use exactly the same words as Alvy and Annie have exchanged in a preceding scene out in California. Art may imitate life, or, Allen seems to imply, vice versa.

Not all his contrivances survived. Eric Lax describes a shot of Alvy in Times Square, 'torn over what to do about Annie, who has gone to California. He looks up at the sign that flashes the news in lights around the top of the Allied Chemical Tower. Instead of news, there is a message: "What are you doing, Alvy? Go to California. It's okay. She loves you." [Allen] hated the scene so much, he drove up to a reservoir and threw the reels in.'[35]

CULTURAL STEREOTYPES

When Allison Portchnik first meets Alvy Singer at a fund-raiser for Democratic candidate Adlai Stevenson, she tells him that she is in the midst of her thesis on 'Political Commitment in Twentieth Century

Literature'. Alvy responds with a Joycean stream of thought about the New York Left that, in her own words, reduces Allison to 'a cultural stereotype'. Unlike a cliché, a stereotype is by no means a pejorative term in the world of Woody Allen. A stereotype defines a certain kind of person, and supplies the director with a methodology for approaching his characters. The humour stems from our familiarity with individuals who in some way resemble those 'stereotypes' we see on screen.

Such stereotypes, not all of them left-wing, form the substance of several Allen films. In *Manhattan*, Mary (Diane Keaton) flays Woody Allen's Ike with her intellectual condescension when they meet in an art gallery. Ike dismisses a steel cube, and Mary says, 'It was absolutely brilliant [...] To me it was very textural. You know what I mean? It was perfectly integrated and it had a marvellous kind of negative capability.' It's as though she were taking revenge for Alvy's patronising remarks when she first meets *him* in *Annie Hall*: 'The medium [of photography] enters in as a condition of the art form itself [...] You need a set of aesthetic guidelines to put in social perspective, I think.'

This pretentious patter can be heard any day of the week at a New York publisher's party or Soho gallery preview. Max von Sydow's Frederick in *Husbands and Wives* pontificates in much the same idiom, and *Love and Death* from start to finish remains a coruscating satire on Russian literature and the intellectual baggage we have attached to it. Indeed Allen lampoons just such a publisher's party when Alvy's wife Robin steers him through a room full of instant celebrities in the literary world. 'Is that Paul Goodman? No. And be nice to the host,' she cautions him, 'because he's publishing my book. Hi, Doug! Douglas Wyatt. "A Foul Rag and Bone Shop of the Heart".'

Name-dropping undoubtedly features as one of Woody Allen's seven deadliest sins. The professor standing in line behind Alvy and Annie for *The Sorrow and the Pity* savages Fellini, followed by Samuel Beckett and Marshall McLuhan. The female reporter for *Rolling Stone* manages to shower Alvy in a couple of minutes with references to Bob Dylan, Mick Jagger, the Stones, Rosicrucianism, and Kafka. 'Art in general,' says the director, 'and show-business, is full to the brim of people who talk, talk, talk, talk.'[36]

He himself commits that very sin, of course, and *Annie Hall*, for all its brilliance, suffers from its profusion of cultural references and asides (see Glossary), by comparison with another 70s masterpiece, *Scenes from a Marriage*, which contains not a single contemporary allusion. An audience aged between 18 and 26, say, will miss many of Allen's fleeting glances at the gossip and icons of the mid-70s. Each of his 'New York' movies – *Annie Hall*, *Manhattan*, *Hannah and Her Sisters* and *Manhattan Murder Mystery* – cannot pretend to a universal impact for those unfamiliar with Allen's name-dropping. It may be a limiting factor, but for those of us in the know it offers a sense of belonging, as if to a club, or a favourite milieu.

Southern Californians are easily served up as cultural stereotypes by Allen. Tony Lacey, the record producer clad forever in white and a plastic smile, drops only a few names but in the amorphous texture of his conversation embodies the lifestyle of prosperous entertainment figures in Los Angeles. Snatches of dialogue are overheard by Alvy as they observe Lacey's party: 'All the good meetings are taken', 'We're gonna operate together', or 'Not only is he a great agent, but he really gives good meetings.'

Stereotypical behaviour works on a domestic level too. The Hall family, with their layers of cool wealth and prejudice, can be found reincarnated in the family created by Arthur and Eve in *Interiors*, and in less cohesive fashion in films like *September*, *Another Woman* and *Alice*. The Singer family, loud, warm-hearted, Jewish, and metropolitan to the core, have their relatives in *Radio Days*, *The Purple Rose of Cairo*, *Broadway Danny Rose* and *Oedipus Wrecks*.

A PERENNIAL APPEAL

Both *Annie Hall* and *Manhattan* feature Woody Allen as an egocentric, who pays the price for his complexes and obsessions. When Annie criticises him for being an island unto himself, like New York City, Alvy retorts sarcastically, 'I can't enjoy myself unless everybody is. If one guy is starving someplace, that puts a crimp in my evening.'

Beyond the laughter and the seductive images of New York, *Annie Hall* exerts a perennial appeal because of Allen's willingness – even eagerness – to share his most intimate experiences with us, the cinema audience. On one level, this means conceding his dislike of driving cars. On another, it implies his genuinely felt identification with artists like Kafka, Dostoevsky and Bergman. 'I think I have all the symptoms and problems that their characters are occupied with: an obsession with death, an obsession with God or the lack of God, the question of why we are here. Almost all of my work is autobiographical – exaggerated but true.'[37]

To audiences in the late 70s, Diane Jacobs's comment rang true: 'We are more interested in Alvy and Annie because they may be Woody Allen and Diane Keaton; and we like Mr Allen and Ms Keaton the better because they may be the lovable Alvy and Annie.'[38] Film buffs seeing the film in the late 90s may think more spontaneously of Allen's embarrassing court appearances after his break-up with Mia Farrow. But the offscreen romance between Allen and Keaton deserves to rank alongside such productive attachments as Antonioni and Monica Vitti, Sternberg and Dietrich, and Bergman and Liv Ullmann. Like Bergman, Woody Allen tailors his roles for those he knows and feels close to. For better or worse, his films draw their nourishment from his own everyday life. As he says himself, 'I hate reality. And, you know, unfortunately it's the only place where we can get a good steak dinner.'[39]

Indeed *Annie Hall* revolves around Allen himself to an exclusive degree. He appears in every scene, and his reactions to people and incidents form the very fabric of the film. Because his talent lies in his verbal repartee, he can be tolerated for long periods on screen; comedians who rely on physical and visual gags tend to pall after a while unless their antics are contrasted with more mundane characters in unexceptional situations.

Not even the great silent comedians, not even Jacques Tati, were so omnipresent in their films as Woody Allen is in *Annie Hall*. The 'dull' moments in the Marx Brothers productions, for example, were those involving the romantic leads. Alvy Singer crowds every frame. When Annie visits her psychiatrist, there's Alvy on the other side of the split screen (the larger portion, too) visiting his. When his parents are seen squabbling during the 40s, there's Alvy watching in the background with his pals. The comparative box-office failure of Allen's chamber cinema – films like *Interiors*, *September*, *Another Woman*, even *Alice* – can be attributed to the absence of the audience's favourite comedian. As he himself concedes, 'I'm forever struggling to deepen myself and to take a more profound path, but what comes easiest to me is light entertainment.'[40]

Paradoxically, although Alvy Singer features like a constant factor, he is rarely seen alone in the film. In the very last shot, after Annie has said farewell, he does turn away down West 63rd Street with his head hunched into his shoulders, a pathetic figure who seems at a loss what to do with his life. And a second intriguing moment of solitude follows an argument with Annie outside their apartment. Alvy asks some passers-by how they cope with sex problems and relationships, and then without warning crosses into the open road to pat the nose of a police horse patrolling the area. The gesture can be interpreted as an amusing comment on Alvy's inability to function with human beings, but it also has a tender, almost private tinge as if to underline that, despite his aggressive, domineering way with women, Alvy possesses a heart of gold.

As it recedes into folk memory, *Annie Hall* jostles with *Manhattan* as Woody Allen's best-loved film. For once the Academy Award for Best Picture did not lie, acknowledging a film that had not only found a large and enthusiastic public, but that had also dared to take risks with its narrative technique and its first-person intimacy which had until then been the province of European directors. When the *Variety International Film Guide* celebrated its twenty-fifth anniversary in 1987, a poll among its correspondents around the world found Allen with two similar, often to be confused films (*Manhattan* and *Annie Hall*) in the 'Top Ten'. In 1995, however, a *Time Out* poll for the Best Film of All Time, conducted among directors and film personalities, saw Allen's star wane completely. Not a single title by him figured in the top hundred titles. Among readers of that magazine, *Manhattan* came seventeenth, although on its first appearance it had not proved so appealing at the box-office as *Annie Hall*.

'It massages the prejudice of the middle class,' says Allen himself of his most popular film. 'It's nothing to be ashamed of but nothing special. It's still the area of romantic comedy and "relationships", which I mean pejoratively, not relationships like *Anna Karenina* and *The Red and the Black*.' [41] He set out, however, with loftier ambitions: 'I said to myself, "I think I will try and make some deeper film and not be as funny in the same way [as *Sleeper* and *Love and Death*]. And maybe there will be other values that will emerge, that will be interesting or nourishing for the audience." And it worked out very well.' [42]

GLOSSARY OF CULTURAL REFERENCES
. . . .

Balzac, Honoré de (1799–1850). French novelist who completed some eighty novels in the 'Human Comedy' series, portraying aspects of nineteenth-century French life. Alvy refers to his prolific output after enjoying his first orgasm with Annie: 'As Balzac said, there goes another novel…'

Beekman, The. Cinema on Second Avenue between 65th and 66th Streets, where most Woody Allen films have received their opening run. It features at the beginning and end of *Annie Hall.*

Beowulf. Anglo-Saxon poem, written about 720, about a German folk hero, Beowulf, who fights in Denmark and becomes king of the Geats before perishing in a fight with a dragon. The only surviving epic of its type and era, it is frequently prescribed for Eng. Lit classes. 'Just don't take any class where they make you read *Beowulf,*' cautions Alvy when Annie is considering adult education classes.

Bergman, Ingmar (1918–). Swedish stage and screen director, whose influence on his work Allen has always acknowledged and embraced.

Buckley, William F. Right-wing political commentator and editor of the *National Review.* When Alvy finds a copy of the magazine on a table in Annie's apartment, he says sarcastically, 'Why don't you get William F. Buckley to kill the spider [in your bathroom]?' The *National Review,* incidentally, is located on the porno shelves in a scene in *Bananas.*

Capote, Truman (Truman Streckfus Parsons, 1924–84). Author of *Breakfast at Tiffany's* and *In Cold Blood,* and a notorious dandy of his time. 'And there's the winner of the Truman Capote look-alike contest,' says Alvy as a fastidiously dressed man strolls past them in Manhattan.

Catcher in the Rye, The. Novel by J. D. Salinger that caused a huge stir when it appeared in 1951, and later featured in the Eng. Lit. syllabus. It's the first book whose ownership is disputed when Alvy and Annie start to break up.

Cavett, Dick. American TV talk show host, at the peak of his popularity in the late 60s and early 70s. Friend of Woody Allen for more than thirty years. Seen in a clip of his own show with Alvy as a guest.

Chaplin, Charles (1889–1977). Woody Allen regards him as probably the greatest comedian in the history of the cinema. Subtle reference to him in scene outside the Beekman, when Alvy turns to camera and says, 'I need a large polo mallet' to fell an unwanted fan; Chaplin often used a polo mallet on his adversaries.

Cheech and Chong. Cheech Marin and Thomas Chong form a zany Chinese/Mexican comedy team, forever on the road and into sex, drugs and rock 'n' roll. Alvy refers to the pseudo-fans pestering him outside the Beekman as 'two guys named Cheech'.

Cooper, Alice. Male rock star at his peak during the 70s. 'I was at an Alice Cooper thing when six people were rushed to the hospital with bad vibes,' deadpans Alvy in response to Pam's reference to the Stones concert at Altamount.

Death in Venice. Novella written by German author Thomas Mann in 1913 (and filmed by Luchino Visconti in 1971). 'What's so great about New York,' asks Annie. 'I mean, it's a dying city. You read *Death in Venice*.'

Denial of Death, The, by Ernest Becker and *Death and Western Thought*, by Jacques Choron. Two volumes picked out by Alvy in a bookshop as gifts for Annie. 'I'm obsessed with death, I think,' stutters Alvy. 'Big thing with me…'

Diamond, Legs. Gangster in Chicago during the Prohibition era. In 1959 Budd Boetticher directed *The Rise and Fall of Legs Diamond*, starring Ray Danton. Tony Lacey proudly informs Alvy and Annie that his Beverly Hills home had once been owned by Diamond.

Eddy, Nelson (1901–67). Concert singer who co-starred with Jeanette MacDonald in a series of winsome screen musicals during the 30s and 40s. Yet another previous inhabitant of the lavish house now occupied by record producer Tony Lacey.

Face to Face. Film made by Ingmar Bergman in 1975 for Swedish TV, and released theatrically in an abridged version in the United States and elsewhere during 1976. Stars Liv Ullmann and Erland Josephson in a drama about a psychiatrist who finds her own mind crumbling. Alvy decides not to see it after Annie arrives two minutes late at the Beekman.

Fellini, Federico (1920–93). Italian director whose films blended autobiographical experiences with fantasy and social comment. Thanks to films like *La Strada*, *La Dolce Vita*, *8½* and *Amarcord*, Fellini became extremely popular in the United States, where he won several Oscars. The academic bore standing behind Alvy and Annie on line at the New Yorker denigrates Fellini.

Fire Island. Resort area off the coast of Long Island, notorious in the 70s for its nude bathing and weekend sex parties, both gay and straight. 'They're back from Fire Island,' says Alvy as he sees a young couple nuzzling each other, 'They're sort of giving it a chance – you know what I mean?'

Geller, Uri. Performer whose self-proclaimed ability to move objects by force of mental projection fascinated TV audiences in the 70s, and who was regarded with either cynicism or awe. 'Uri Geller must be on the premises someplace,' says Alvy, in an ironic comment on the fact that guests are wearing white at Tony Lacey's party and seem to come together as if by magic.

Ghosts. Play by Henrik Ibsen first published in 1881, so controversial that it received its world premiere in Chicago, rather than Oslo. Robin, Alvy's second wife, refers to Oswald, a character of failing creativity with whom Ibsen himself in old age was compared.

Godfather, The. Gangster film directed by Francis Ford Coppola from the novel by Mario Puzo and released in 1972. Alvy tells Annie that he has met the 'cast of *The Godfather*' outside the Beekman cinema.

Hefner, Hugh (1926–). Founder of *Playboy* magazine in 1953, and thus of a 'liberated' lifestyle for men which led to the opening of Playboy Clubs around the world. Alvy's friend Rob claims that he lives 'right next to Hefner' in Los Angeles.

Holiday, Billie (Eleanora Gough McKay, 1915–59). US jazz singer, who brought a flair for blues to all her work, especially with swing bands.

Illusion, Grand. (La Grande illusion). French anti-war film, made in 1936 by Jean Renoir. At a Hollywood party, a girl tells Alvy and Annie that he has just seen *Grand Illusion*. 'That's a great film if you're high,' interjects a man on a neighbouring sofa.

James, Henry (1843–1916). American novelist whose books include *The Portrait of a Lady, Washington Square, The Ambassadors, The Bostonians* and *The Golden Bowl*. Alvy refers to his supernatural story *The Turn of the Screw*, which was made into a film in 1961 by Jack Clayton under the title of *The Innocents*.

Kafka, Franz (1883–1924). Czech novelist whose works deal with the persecution of the individual by overwhelming bureaucratic and often abstract forces. 'Sex with you is a Kafkaesque experience,' claims the reporter from *Rolling Stone*, 'and I mean that as a compliment.'

Kissinger, Henry (1923–). German-born US diplomat and academic, who served as Nixon's Secretary of State, 1973–77. When he hears that record producer Tony Lacey has graduated from Harvard, Alvy responds: 'Listen, Harvard makes mistakes too, you know. Kissinger taught there.'

Leopold and Loeb. Two young homosexuals who, in 1924, kidnapped and then murdered a youth to demonstrate Nietzschean theory. Their story was fictionalised on screen in Hitchcock's *Rope* and in Richard Fleischer's *Compulsion*. In conversation with the reporter from *Rolling Stone*, Alvy mutters, 'I think there's too much burden placed on the orgasm, you know, to make up for empty areas in life.' When the girl asks him who said that, Alvy replies: 'It might have been Leopold and Loeb.'

Manson family. In 1969, Charles Manson led a cult that murdered the actress Sharon Tate and several others. Jailed, Manson, with his messianic hairdo and burning stare, remained a closet idol for psychopaths. In a bedroom exchange with Robin, his second wife, Alvy lists the Manson family as one of the perils of leaving Manhattan and living 'in the country' (i.e. anywhere from the city limits to infinity).

Marx, Groucho (1890–1977). American comedian and senior member of the Marx Brothers team. From 1947 to 1962 he hosted his own quiz show on TV, *You Bet Your Life*. Alvy refers to his joke about not belonging to any club that would have him as a member.

Masters and Johnson. US team of researchers (then married, now divorced) into sexual habits among Americans. Their published works proved best-sellers, notably in the 70s, and their clinic attracted innumerable couples. Rob sees a couple embracing at Tony Lacey's party and says, 'I think they just came back from Masters and Johnson.'

McLuhan, Marshall (1911–80). Canadian theorist specialising in communications, who coined such phrases as 'the medium is the message' and 'the global village'. Produced by Alvy from behind a film poster in the lobby of the Beekman, just four years before his actual death.

Medea. Play by Euripides about a woman who murdered the bride of Jason and her own children. Alvy admits to a passer-by in the street that he is jealous, 'a little bit like Medea', of Annie living with another man in California.

Munchkinland. Reference to the midgets, or 'Munchkins' in *The Wizard of Oz*. Alvy dismisses the Southern Californian lifestyle as 'Munchkinland', while arguing with Annie. It might also be a snide comment at the expense of Tony Lacey/Paul Simon, who is short of stature.

Nicholson, Jack, and *Huston, Anjelica.* Screen stars whose long-term affair marked them out as a charismatic couple. In *Annie Hall,* record producer Tony Lacey invites Alvy and Annie up to the Hotel Pierre to meet 'Jack and Anjelica'.

Plath, Sylvia (1932–63). American poet who committed suicide in England after establishing a reputation for intense, desolate verse. Annie finds her poetry 'neat', while Alvy dismisses her as an 'interesting poetess whose tragic suicide was misinterpreted as romantic, by the college-girl mentality'.

Popular Mechanics. Monthly magazine beloved of both engineering nerds and teenage science buffs. 'I can't get with any religion that advertises in *Popular Mechanics*,' snaps Alvy when he's talking with the female reporter from *Rolling Stone.*

Rockwell, Norman (1894–1978). American painter who depicted scenes from the domestic life of Middle America on innumerable covers for the *Saturday Evening Post.* 'What did you do, grow up in a Norman Rockwell painting?' asks Alvy when he first meets Annie Hall.

Rolling Stone. American magazine covering the popular music scene, and host to some great reportage (e.g. Michael Herr's dispatches from Vietnam). Alvy's girlfriend Pam serves as a reporter for the paper.

Rolling Stones, The. Rock band formed in 1962 under Mick Jagger, whose enduring popularity has not compromised their rebellious image. 'The most charismatic event I covered,' recalls Pam in *Annie Hall,* 'was Mick's birthday when the Stones played Madison Square Garden.'

Rosicrucians. Group of early seventeenth-century philosophers who believed in the power of alchemy and the occult. Alvy's girlfriend (played by Shelley Duvall) pronounces herself a Rosicrucian at the Maharishi's rally. The movement has attracted some interesting converts, including French composer Erik Satie.

Sinatra, Frank (1915–). Singer and screen actor who pops up in one of Annie's dreams and is transmogrified into Alvy's bespectacled features as he tries to suffocate her with a pillow.

Sorrow and the Pity, The. Swiss-German TV co-production, running four and a half hours, documenting life in Clermont-Ferrand and the Auvergne regions of central France during the Occupation. Shot in 1969 and released theatrically in the United States three years later. Two brief clips from the film appear in *Annie Hall.* 'I'm not in the mood to see a four-hour documentary on Nazis,' sighs Annie.

Stevenson, Adlai (1900–65). US Democrat politician, twice defeated by Eisenhower in the race for the White House. Alvy's first wife, Allison Portchnik, is a campaign worker for Stevenson, and Allen performs in aid of Stevenson's cause.

Thalia, The. Upper West Side art-house cinema, now closed. Scene of one of Alvy and Annie's last encounters on screen.

Trigger. Cowboy Roy Rogers' horse, which appeared with him in most of his Westerns. When Tony Lacey is dropping names of celebrities who have owned his house in Beverly Hills, Alvy mutters under his breath that Trigger probably occupied it also.

NOTES

· ·

1 Robert Benayoun, *Woody Allen: Beyond Words* (London: Pavilion, 1986).
2 Diane Jacobs, *The Magic of Woody Allen* (London: Robson, 1982).
3 Eric Lax, *Woody Allen, A Biography* (London: Jonathan Cape, 1991).
4 Stig Björkman (in conversation with), *Woody Allen on Woody Allen* (London: Faber and Faber, 1994).
5 Jacobs, *The Magic of Woody Allen*.
6 Marshall Brickman, quoted from sleeve notes for the laser disc of *Annie Hall*, published by Voyager Press/The Criterion Collection (CC1231L, 1990).
7 Lax, *Woody Allen*.
8 Brickman, sleeve notes for *Annie Hall*.
9 Björkman, *Woody Allen*.
10 Ibid.
11 Brickman, sleeve notes for *Annie Hall*.
12 Björkman, *Woody Allen*.
13 Allen Eyles, *The Marx Brothers, Their World of Comedy* (London: Tantivy Press; New York: A. S. Barnes & Co., 1966).
14 Benayoun, *Woody Allen*.
15 Benny Green, in *The Spectator* (quoted on jacket for *Without Feathers*, London: Elm Tree Books/Hamish Hamilton, 1976).
16 Lax, *Woody Allen*.
17 Björkman, *Woody Allen*.
18 Lax, *Woody Allen*.
19 Björkman, *Woody Allen*.
20 Lax, *Woody Allen*.

21 Jacobs, *The Magic of Woody Allen*.
22 Björkman, *Woody Allen*.
23 Lax, *Woody Allen*.
24 Ibid.
25 Ibid.
26 Allen's early friend Judy Henske, the folksinger, came from Chippewa Falls. 'That's where I got the name for Annie Hall's hometown.' (Quoted in Lax, *Woody Allen*.)
27 Quoted in Graham Flashner, *Everything You Always Wanted to Know about Woody Allen, A Fun Quiz Book for Woody Allen Fans* (London: Robson, 1979).
28 Benayoun, *Woody Allen*.
29 Allen's dislike of virtually all flora and fauna also surfaces in *Stardust Memories*, when he tries to dispose of a pigeon ('They're rats with wings') with a fire extinguisher.
30 Jacobs, *The Magic of Woody Allen*.
31 Björkman, *Woody Allen*.
32 Jacobs, *The Magic of Woody Allen*.
33 Björkman, *Woody Allen*.
34 Jacobs, *The Magic of Woody Allen*.
35 Lax, *Woody Allen*.
36 Björkman, *Woody Allen*.
37 Lax, *Woody Allen*.
38 Jacobs, *The Magic of Woody Allen*.
39 Björkman, *Woody Allen*.
40 Lax, *Woody Allen*.
41 Ibid.
42 Björkman, *Woody Allen*.

CREDITS

· ·

Annie Hall

USA
1977
Distributor
United Artists
Production company
United Artists Corporation
A Jack Rollins-Charles H.
Joffe Production
Executive producer
Robert Greenhut
Producer
Charles H. Joffe
Associate producer
Fred T. Gallo
Production manager
Robert Greenhut
Production assistants
Chris Cronyn, Beth Rudin,
Stuart Smiley
Director
Woody Allen
Assistant director
Fred T. Gallo
Screenplay
Woody Allen, Marshall
Brickman
Script supervisor
Kay Chapin
**Photography (colour by
DeLuxe)**
Gordon Willis
Camera operator
Fred Schuler
**Los Angeles camera
operator**
Don Thorin
Stills
Brian Hamill

Songs
'Seems Like Old Times' by
Carmen Lombardo (music),
John Jacob Loeb (lyrics);
'It Had To Be You' by
Isham Jones (music), Gus
Kahn (lyrics); 'A Hard Way
to Go' performed by Tim
Weisberg; 'Christmas
Medley' performed by The
Do-Re-Mi Children's
Chorus; 'Sleepy Lagoon' by
Jack Lawrence, Eric Coates,
performed by Tommy
Dorsey
**Diane Keaton's
accompanist**
Artie Butler
Editor
Ralph Rosenblum
Art director
Mel Bourne
Set decorators
Robert Drumheller, Justin
Scoppa Jr.
**Los Angeles set
decorator**
Barbara Krieger
Animated sequences
Chris Ishii
Titles
Computer Opticals
Costume designer
Ruth Morley
Clothing designs
Ralph Lauren
Make-up artist
Fern Buchner
Los Angeles make-up
John Inzerella
Sound editor
Dan Sable/Magnofex
Sound mixer
James Sabat
**Los Angeles sound
mixer**
James Pilcher

Re-recording mixer
Jack Higgins
93 minutes
8,372 feet

Woody Allen
Alvy Singer
Diane Keaton
Annie Hall
Tony Roberts
Rob
Carol Kane
Allison
Paul Simon
Tony Lacey
Shelley Duvall
Pam
Janet Margolin
Robin
Christopher Walken
Duane Hall
Donald Symington
Dad Hall
Helen Ludlam
Grammy Hall
Mordecai Lawner
Alvy's dad
Joan Newman
Alvy's mom
Jonathan Munk
Alvy, aged 9
Ruth Volner
Alvy's aunt
Martin Rosenblatt
Alvy's uncle
Hy Ansel
Joey Nichols
Rashel Novikoff
Aunt Tessie
Russell Horton
Man in theatre line
Marshall McLuhan
Himself
Christine Jones
Dorrie
Mary Boylan
Miss Reed

Wendy Girard
Janet
John Doumanian
Coke fiend
Bob Maroff
Rick Petrucelli
Men outside theatre
Lee Callahan
Ticket seller at theatre
Chris Gampel
Doctor
Mark Lenard
Navy officer
Dan Ruskin
Comedian at rally
John Glover
Actor boyfriend
Bernie Styles
Comic's agent
Johnny Haymer
Comic
Ved Bandhu
Maharishi
John Dennis Johnston
Los Angeles policeman
Lauri Bird
Tony Lacey's girlfriend
Jim McKrell
Jeff Goldblum
William Callaway
Roger Newman
Alan Landers
Jean Sarah Frost
Lacey party guests

Vince O'Brien
Hotel doctor
Humphrey Davis
Alvy's psychiatrist
Veronica Radburn
Annie's psychiatrist
Robin Mary Paris
Actress in rehearsal
Charles Levin
Actor in rehearsal
Wayne Carson
Rehearsal stage manager
Michael Karm
Rehearsal director
Petronia Johnson
Shaun Casey
Tony's dates at nightclub
Ricardo Bertoni
Michael Aronin
Waiters at nightclub
Lou Picetti
Loretta Tupper
James Burge
Shelly Hack
Albert Ottenheimer
Paula Trueman
Street strangers
Beverly D'Angelo
Actress in Rob's TV show
Tracey Walter
Actor in Rob's TV show

David Wier
Keith Dentice
Susan Mellinger
Hamit Perezic
James Balter
Eric Gould
Amy Levitan
Alvy's classmates
Gary Allen
Frank Vohs
Sybil Bowan
Margaretta Warwick
Schoolteachers
Lucy Lee Flippen
Waitress at health food restaurant
Gary Muledeer
Man at health food restaurant
Sigourney Weaver
Passer-by outside theatre
Walter Bernstein
Annie's date outside theatre
[and uncredited]
Dick Cavett
Himself

Credits checked by Markku Salmi. The print of *Annie Hall* in the National Film and Television Archive was acquired specially for the 360 project from Utd. International Pictures (UK).

Annie Hall is available on VHS in the UK on the Warner Home Video label.

BIBLIOGRAPHY

Adler, Bill, and Feinman, Jeffrey. *Woody Allen, Clown Prince of American Humor* (New York: Pinnacle, 1975).

Allen, Woody. *Four Films of Woody Allen: Annie Hall, Interiors, Manhattan, Stardust Memories* (New York: Random House, 1982; London: Faber & Faber, 1983). Screenplays.

Allen, Woody. *Getting Even* (New York: Random House, 1971).

Allen, Woody. *Without Feathers* (New York: Random House, 1975; London: Elm Tree Books/Hamish Hamilton, 1976).

Allen, Woody. *Side Effects* (New York: Random House, 1980).

Benayoun, Robert. *Woody Allen: Beyond Words* (London: Pavilion/Michael Joseph, 1986, translated from the French by Alexander Walker).

Björkman, Stig (in conversation with). *Woody Allen on Woody Allen* (London: Faber & Faber, 1994).

De Navacelle, Thierry. *Woody Allen on Location* (New York: William Morrow, 1987).

Flashner, Graham. *Everything You Always Wanted to Know about Woody, A Fun Quiz Book for Woody Allen Fans* (London: Robson, 1989).

Guthrie, Lee. *Woody Allen, A Biography* (London and New York: Drake, 1978).

Hamill, Brian. *Woody Allen at Work, The Photographs of Brian Hamill* (New York: Harry N. Abrams, 1995).

Hirsch, Foster. *Love, Death, and the Meaning of Life* (New York: McGraw-Hill, 1981).

Jacobs, Diane. *The Magic of Woody Allen* (London: Robson, 1982).

Lax, Eric. *On Being Funny: Woody Allen and His Comedy* (London: Hamish Hamilton/Elm Tree Books, 1976).

Lax, Eric. *Woody Allen, A Biography* (London: Jonathan Cape, 1991).

McCann, Graham. *Woody Allen* (Cambridge: Polity Press, 1990).

McKnight, Gerald. *Woody Allen: Joking Aside* (New York: Howard & Wyndham; London: W. H. Allen, 1982).

Palmer, Miles. *Woody Allen, An Illustrated Biography* (London: Proteus, 1980).

Yacowar, Maurice. *Loser Take All, The Comic Art of Woody Allen* (New York: Ungar, 1979).

ALSO PUBLISHED

An Actor's Revenge
Ian Breakwell

L'Atalante
Marina Warner

The Big Heat
Colin MacArthur

Blackmail
Tom Ryall

Boudu Saved from Drowning
Richard Boston

Brief Encounter
Richard Dyer

Citizen Kane
Laura Mulvey

Double Indemnity
Richard Schickel

42nd Street
J. Hoberman

The Ghost and Mrs Muir
Frieda Grafe

Greed
Jonathan Rosenbaum

Gun Crazy
Jim Kitses

In a Lonely Place
Dana Polan

It's a Gift
Simon Louvish

Lolita
Richard Corliss

Meet Me in St. Louis
Gerald Kaufman

Napoléon
Nelly Kaplan

Odd Man Out
Dai Vaughan

Olympia
Taylor Downing

Queen Christina
Marcia Landy and Amy Villarejo

Rocco and his Brothers
Sam Rohdie

The Seventh Seal
Melvyn Bragg

Singin' in the Rain
Peter Wollen

Stagecoach
Edward Buscombe

Things to Come
Christopher Frayling

Went the Day Well?
Penelope Houston

Wild Strawberries
Philip and Kersti French

The Wizard of Oz
Salman Rushdie

If you would like further information about future BFI Film Classics or about other books on film, media and popular culture from BFI Publishing, please write to:

BFI Film Classics
British Film Institute
21 Stephen Street
London
W1P 2LN